THE YEAR IN
TENNIS 2000

Neil Harman | International Tennis Federation | Universe

First published in the United States of America in 2000 by
Universe Publishing • A division of Rizzoli International Publications, Inc.
300 Park Avenue South New York, NY 10010

©2000 The International Tennis Federation • Bank Lane, Roehampton
London, sw15 5XZ, England

2001 2002 2003 | 10 9 8 7 6 5 4 3 2 1

Library of Congress Card Number • 2001086093

Printed in England

CONTENTS

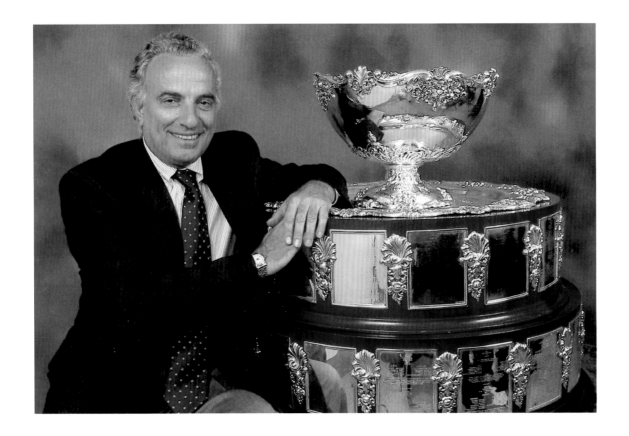

PRESIDENT'S MESSAGE

The 2000 Davis Cup by NEC will be unforgettable for many reasons. In dramatic fashion, Spain won its first Davis Cup title, defeating Australia to become only the tenth nation to win the Cup in its more than one-hundred-year history. Record audiences watched the Final around the world and, in Spain, over twenty-two million people followed their country's fortunes with a market share of over 55 percent watching the presentation of the coveted trophy on Sunday. The Davis Cup website posted a record-breaking forty-seven million page views in 2000 and this important tool continues to grow and prosper. The Final was the culmination of a year that saw 136 eager nations enter this historic competition. The decisive match between two of tennis's most talented young stars, Juan Carlos Ferrero and Lleyton Hewitt, was of a very high standard. Their grit and determination during this encounter made it plain to all who watched that winning the Cup means as much to this new generation as it has to every great player of the last century.

It is clear that Davis Cup arouses unprecedented passion in both competitors and spectators. Many players cite a Davis Cup experience as a pivotal moment in their careers, a springboard that launches them on to other achievements. In 2000, the new stars of the game ensured that the traditions of this great event, embodied by the distinctive silver punch bowl, will be maintained into the twenty-first century as they lined up alongside their experienced teammates to strive for sporting glory for their country.

Congratulations to the author, Neil Harman, who has undertaken extensive research and carried out numerous interviews to compile this comprehensive and entertaining book, which tells the stories of this year's nail-biting triumphs and losses, outpourings of team spirit, and excellent tennis. Some wonderful photographs by some of the best tennis photographers in the world accompany the text, bringing additional color to the book. The highs and lows of this year's competition have included the USA's extraordinary 3–2 victories over Zimbabwe and the Czech Republic before its subsequent downfall to Spain; Brazil's sensational victory over 1999 finalists France in the opening round; and Australia's heart-stopping 3–2 victory over Switzerland. My congratulations to Spain and to Australia, who reached the top of the Davis Cup ladder in 2000, and to the other 134 nations who played Davis Cup this year. We appreciate your participation in this important competition and we wish you well in your campaign for the 2001 Davis Cup.

Francesco Ricci Bitti • President • International Tennis Federation

FOREWORD

Winning the Davis Cup is the greatest feeling I have ever had in my life. I have always dreamed of this moment. Nothing compares to what I felt in the stadium when Juan Carlos won his last match, and to what I now feel weeks later when the people of Spain and the media look at me as a hero. I have had great moments in my career, but none of them will ever mean the same for me as winning the Davis Cup for the first time in Spain's history.

When I was a kid, during the weekends, I used to play with my friends what we called "Davis Cup." We tried to emulate players like Lendl, Becker, Edberg, McEnroe, or Noah. Later, when I was sixteen, the Spanish Tennis Federation gave me the chance to travel and train with the Davis Cup team. Today, it is a great honor for me to write the foreword for the Davis Cup Yearbook.

One thing I would like to mention is the great union that existed among the Spanish team, which gave Spain its triumph. A revolutionary idea of our president Agustin Pujol became a success. No one could imagine that a team with four captains could ever work. Duarte, Perlas, Vilaro, and Avendano demonstrated how to be honest and professional. They were the ones to show the others how to work together. The team also incorporated the doctor, the physical trainers, and all the assistants. It took all their efforts for Spain to capture a title it could not win in one hundred years of competition.

The success is not only for Balcells, Costa, Ferrero, and Corretja, it is for all the Spanish Tennis Armada, from the present players to the big legends like Arilla, Gisbert, and Orantes, who gave us all the support we needed to win.

I would not like to forget the fair play I have experienced in all the rounds against Italy, Russia, USA, and Australia. This is one of the things that makes the sport of tennis so special.

Davis Cup is different. It is the best way your country can identify with you as a player, and the best way you can identify with the crowd and the people of your country. Their support, on and off the court, is fundamental. The cities of Murcia, Malaga, Santander, and especially Barcelona (my hometown) will always remain in the deepest place of my heart.

It has been, with no doubt, the biggest success in tennis for Spain. I wish to live it again.

Alex Corretja

MEN OF VISION

"THE GIFT OF THE CUP WAS ONE OF THOSE HAPPY INSPIRATIONS—THEY COME
TO MEN OF VISION—WHICH IN WAYS RARELY UNDERSTANDABLE AT THE TIME, ARE
AFTERWARDS FOUND TO HAVE LEFT THEIR MARK ON THE CURRENT OF HUMAN
LIFE AND RELATIONSHIPS."

Thus was penned an editorial in the British publication *Lawn Tennis and Badminton*
reflecting in the 1940s on the life and legacy of Dwight Filley Davis. It is to that vision that
136 countries paid due homage in 2000—a momentous year of playing for what was called
the International Lawn Tennis Challenge Trophy before it became known as the Davis Cup.

From Andre Agassi's first serve in Harare in February to Juan Carlos Ferrero's clinching
backhand eleven months later, it was a privilege to catalogue the ebb and flow of a competition
that, for its (exceedingly) negligible number of would-be tinkerers and detractors, has few
equals in modern sport. And in lawn tennis, a sport that requires bouts of intense solitude and
selfish sacrifice, it is the one annual opportunity to be part of something different, to represent
your country, to take wholesome pride in something more than personal achievement.

Those ideals were cherished in Barcelona in December as the team of Ferrero, Alex Corretja,
Albert Costa, and Juan Balcells carved their names and spirit into Spanish sporting folklore.
It was twenty-one years into the Davis Cup that Spain first entered, a further seventy-nine
before it became the champion nation. The emotional release of their victory is chronicled
elsewhere. Its impact was quite astonishing. One hundred years ago, having accepted the
invitation from Harvard scholar Davis to take part in what certain Boston newspapers called
the World Championship of Tennis, the British Isles team gathered at London's Euston
Station to take the boat train to Liverpool for the sailing to New York. Their names were
Herbert Roper Barrett, Arthur W. Gore, and Ernest D. Black.

Before they left the capital, they were given a private luncheon by the Lawn Tennis
Association and presented with white satin caps, embroidered with the Royal Standard. There,
too, they received a send-off in verse, a parody of Macaulay's "Horatius at the Bridge" in

praise of "the Dauntless Three" who had stepped forward when the famous Doherty brothers, Laurie and Reggie, declined the opportunity to take on the might of the United States.

…for since we lack the brothers twain / What hope to win the cup? / Then spoke out brave Goratius,
   The back court player great;

"Lo, every man upon this earth / Gets beaten soon or late; / And how can man play better
   Than facing fearful odds / For honour and his country, / And the old lawn tennis Gods?

…Then out spake E.D. Niger, / A Yorkshire man was he; / "Lo, I will play the second string,
   And singles play with thee!"

And out spake Roper Barrett, / Of Gipsy club was he: / "I will abide, at right hand side, / In Doubles with E.D."…

And off they went for a 3–0 defeat on the grass courts of the Longwood Cricket Club, in Brookline, Massachusetts. Davis beat Black in four sets in the opening singles; Malcolm Whitman thrashed Gore in straight sets; and Davis and Holcombe Ward defeated Black and Roper Barrett in the doubles.

American tennis writers paid the visitors a series of handsome compliments (how times have changed in one hundred years!). According to Nancy Kriplen's wonderful book *Dwight Davis—The Man and The Cup*, the British team did not lob excessively, did not fuss about line calls, did not worry about stray balls elsewhere on the court, and kept the game moving along quickly by not dawdling between points or "taking elaborate care of themselves between the sets."

That Friday evening began the Davis Cup tradition of the concluding banquet, at which players from both sides, mellowed by good food and wine, toasted each other, the game, and the defining value of international competition. The next morning, the British team left on the train for New York. It was the first of so many journeys—to new and ever-wider frontiers—that have seen the Davis Cup enter a new century.

A hundred years hence and the Spanish and Australian teams from the 2000 Final arrived at the Sunday banquet in the splendor of the Palau de Pedralbes with tales to tell and friendships to define. John Newcombe, the defeated captain, spoke of his immense pride at those who had answered his call to sporting arms across seven years in charge of his team. He spoke of the tears he could well have shed for them that night, the losers, who were not really losers at all.

The Spanish captain Javier Duarte, having made history, was equally impassioned. After the Australians left, the Spanish danced. And danced. And danced some more.

They went on to a disco called Gaslight, where the players ended up onstage, and Ferrero, the lad with the face of a choirboy, performed what a local paper called "un simpatico y discreto striptease." There were shades of Australia's 1999 hero, Mark Philippoussis, in Nice, but without the accompanying female distractions.

By the time the kid presented himself just before noon the next day for a marathon session of interviews, the Davis Cup had done this for him: Sergio Tacchini signed him up for a four-year shirt contract; the tourist office of his home province, Valencia, tabled a bid to become his leading sponsor; Spain's top communications company, Telefonica, offered what it called a "supercontracto"; and the citizens in his hometown of

Onteniente circulated a petition to raise a monument in his honor. Ferrero had dinner that night at McDonald's.

Through the years, this competition has made men and, in equal, dispassionate measure, broken them. The stories of 2000 sit well with those of the past—stories of heroism above and beyond the call of duty, and those moments of sorrow in the face of defeat from which only the strongest spirit recovers.

There were moments of dispute and rancor this year—the disgraceful crowd scene in Santiago, Chile, on April 7, when the home nation led its great rival, Argentina, 1–0. Argentina's Mariano Zabaleta was leading Nicolas Massu in the second singles 7–5, 2–6, 7–6, 3–1, when the crowd started hurling chairs. "I have never been so frightened," recalled Zabaleta, the 1995 world junior number 1. "They were screaming at us. It was more like a soccer crowd than a tennis crowd. I was really upset because my father was there and I was worried for him. We didn't want to stay to play any more. We wanted to go home."

The referee, Tony Hernandez, ruled that play should be resumed on Saturday behind closed doors, but the Argentines refused and returned to Buenos Aires. Hernandez felt the visiting team's safety and security were guaranteed under the new arrangements and declared Chile the winner. Argentina appealed. The winner of the American Zone Group One second round tie would reach the World Group Qualifying Round to be held in July.

The ITF's board of directors upheld the referee's decision but decided neither country should benefit from the shaming furor. Chile was not allowed to advance to their qualifying round tie against Morocco, and Morocco was promoted to the World Group for the first time. (Welcome Hicham Arazi, Karim Alami, and Younes El Aynaoui to the big league.) Chile was also denied a home tie until 2002 for its failure to ensure a safe venue and was fined $47,800—the payment it would have received for winning the tie.

Argentina faced possible relegation to Group Two of the American Zone. And for failing to comply with the referee's instruction to continue to play, Argentina was fined $25,700—the loser's prospective prize money. It left a bitter taste.

As did the resignation of John McEnroe after less than a year as the American captain—a depressingly sad reflection on his inability to commit his leading players to participate. Having arrived in such a blaze of glory and opportunity, he bowed out, making way for his younger brother Patrick.

McEnroe's personal history in the event made his parting such sweet sorrow. He said in December: "Every one has had a say—most of it guesswork—about why I resigned from the American Davis Cup captaincy. It's time to put the record straight.

"I've spoken at length in the past about the set-up of the championship and why I think it needs to change— but this decision went a lot deeper than dates and places. With my six kids, a full schedule on the Seniors Tour, and broadcasting commitments before I was asked to become the captain, a lot of juggling was always going to be part of the total equation.

"From the first trip to Zimbabwe, I found I was getting too stressed out—and not sleeping well in the weeks of Davis Cup. I'm a hyper kind of person at the best of times but this was different and a bit worrying.

"My aim was to try to prolong everyone's enjoyment factor of Davis Cup. I felt I could get Pete Sampras to a better place. I know he feels he wants more respect and I knew he could achieve that with my help.

Andre Agassi had a miraculous comeback in 1999 and I sensed he could hold on to it for a couple more years with the Davis Cup playing a vital part in that. Maybe I could find out the reason why Michael Chang didn't want the Davis Cup any more.

"I was shooting for the stars and had to settle for the moon. Look at Pete this year, he hasn't played much and I basically agree with that—he's done the four majors, seven other tournaments and had he focused more on Davis Cup it would have been a real positive mixture. No one could have foreseen that Andre would be involved in a car accident just before the semifinal against Spain and Jim Courier went and retired when he could have been a real factor for the U.S. there.

"I was extremely uncomfortable being on the court in the situations I was in. I sensed, sitting there, not enough time had passed between John McEnroe the player and John McEnroe the captain. There is nothing worse than sitting through matches and wondering if you really should be there—and how much better you should be doing.

"I think I helped people to a certain level of recognition. When Chris Woodruff looks back on his career, the fifth match in Zimbabwe will go down as one of his greatest moments and I helped him over that hump. Had I not been more encouraging, Pete might have retired with an injury in L.A. against the Czechs. Despite the fact we lost 5–0 in Spain in the semis, Jan-Michael Gambill was playing the finest tennis of his life.

"I couldn't have been more honored and I know there are those who said I should have stuck with it. I gave myself three years and I've gone after one. Maybe the players will turn out now, I don't know. It is much more important to me that the best players play for America and if there is a better chance of that happening without me there, that's fine."

Almost immediately after he heard the news, the president of the International Tennis Federation, Francesco Ricci Bitti, was penning his own thoughts on the subject: "The ITF, the owner and guardian of the century-old Davis Cup, has always been open to consider any legitimate suggestion that can improve the competition. As part of the review process, the Davis Cup committee weighs the pros and cons of any proposal and to date, any suggested change has been thought to have more negatives than positives.

"I would also like to say that player participation in the Davis Cup has traditionally been linked to the relationship that a National Association has with its players. As they do every year, 95 percent of the top players in 2000 found time in their schedule to accept the honor of representing their country in the Davis Cup. This does not suggest a problem with the format of the Davis Cup, but there are always a few individuals for whom the scheduling is difficult.

"Let me point out that while the Davis Cup has a four-week schedule, only the two finalists make a four-week commitment to the competition, while most nations have only a two-week commitment during any given year. This should be looked at in its proper context. The four Grand Slams take only eight weeks of the calendar, while there are over thirty weeks of tournaments on the ATP Tour.

"I am sorry that Mr. McEnroe found his experience as captain unsatisfactory but hope that, when he has a chance to reflect on the year, he will remember the qualities that inspired him as a Davis Cup player and influenced him to accept the position as U.S. Davis Cup captain."

With open minds and open hearts, nothing is beyond the wit of those charged with preserving the future of the sport. The Davis Cup is part of tennis heritage—there are those who have fallen out of love with it, there are those who could not do without it. Look at the face of Lleyton Hewitt as the final master stroke of young Senor Ferrero flew past him on December 10 and tell him that this event doesn't matter any more.

As retiring Australian captain Newcombe said: "I thought that Lleyton's two singles matches in the Final against Costa and Ferrero were what sport's all about, two guys just going at one another. Today, against Ferrero, were two of the future people in the world of tennis playing in a match you just had to applaud. It didn't matter who won the points because they were just great points.

"They are going to be around for another eight to ten years, playing more huge matches against one another. Tennis is going to be the better for it."

With that the Australians bade Spain farewell—"until next year when we win it back hopefully," said Newcombe. In another corner of the room, Alex Corretja dipped his head into the famous punchbowl filled with champagne and drank until he emerged, dribbling and beaming to accept the plaudits of his countrymen.

To his future, we drink heartily. It was that way in 1932, when Great Britain, captained by Herbert Roper Barrett, a player from the original match, defeated France at Roland Garros, the British being inspired by Fred Perry and H. "Bunny" Austin. The great Austin died in August 2000, a month after taking part in the grand Champions' Parade on Wimbledon's Centre Court.

In *For the Love of Tennis*, a glorious tennis anthology, Perry recalls: "On the way back to our hotel, we tastelessly flourished the trophy we had taken away from the French after six years, much to the disgust of the passers-by. That evening, after the official dinner, [Henri] Cochet, swallowing his national sorrow, said: 'Let's go out for a night on the town and take the Cup with us.'

"I said: 'We can't do that.' 'Oh yes we can,' he replied. With a few friends of his, we got the trophy out of the hotel and set off on a tour of the Paris nightclubs. Everywhere we went the band would strike up the 'Marseillaise' followed by 'God Save the King.'

"We would fill the Cup with champagne, everyone would take a drink then it was off to the next club. The celebrations went on all night, and it wasn't until 7 A.M. we got back to our hotel on the Place de la Concorde, carrying the Cup and followed by an orchestra we had picked up along the way with a decidedly mixed gathering of hangers-on.

"I don't suppose the authorities would have approved of their precious trophy going on a grand tour of Parisian nightspots, but the LTA found the Cup where it was supposed to be next morning in time for our Channel crossing home. The whole length of the train journey from Dover to London, people were standing in their back gardens waving to us as we held up the Davis Cup. At Victoria Station, it was chaos. About ten thousand people swarmed the police cordon, grabbed Austin and myself and marched us off on their shoulders."

Goodbye, dear Bunny, gone to join Fred for a game of heavenly doubles. Don't worry, the Davis Cup is still here, safe as ever!

ROUND ONE

USA d. Zimbabwe • *Harare, Zimbabwe* | Czech Republic d. Great Britain • *Ostrava, Czech Republic* |

Spain d. Italy • *Murcia, Spain* | Russia d. Belgium • *Moscow, Russia* | Slovak Republic d. Austria • *Bratislava,*

Slovak Republic | Brazil d. France • *Florianopolis, Brazil* | Germany d. Netherlands • *Leipzig, Germany* |

Australia d. Switzerland • *Zurich, Switzerland* | *matches played February 4–6, 2000*

DAVIS CUP IN THE NEW MILLENNIUM

Inside the Qantas lounge at Perth airport was perched Andre Agassi, crowned the Australian Open champion at Melbourne Park the previous afternoon. On the table in front of him were the dregs of a Bloody Mary, celery stick and all. Agassi's coach, Brad Gilbert, wondered if he wanted another. "Make it a bit spikier," said his charge.

Agassi was a quarter of the way from Melbourne to Zimbabwe and halfway to an extremely relaxed second leg of the journey. He confessed that he had not slept much the previous night, full of the emotions of touching another mountaintop, and that he had trouble believing all that had happened to him since the previous year's French Open.

In truth, many people had trouble believing it, too. Inside eight months, Agassi had won Roland Garros, reached the final of Wimbledon, breezed through the United States Open, reached the final of the ATP Tour World Championships, and been crowned the world number 1. And now he had captured the first major of 2000. The only player to have beaten him on this spree was his old rival, Pete Sampras.

But Agassi was heading for Harare and Sampras wasn't. The high moral ground, as well as the hallowed turf of preeminence over the sport, belonged to the man from Las Vegas.

From the moment John McEnroe became the American Davis Cup captain in September, there was likely to be an apocalypse in the offing. He joked about walking out onto court before the start of the first singles and pulling the umpire from his chair, just to get it over and done with, satiating the media's thirst for a moment of "you cannot be serious"-ness.

When McEnroe named Sampras, Agassi, Todd Martin, and Alex O'Brien as his four-man team for the World Group First Round tie in Zimbabwe, his goal was to deliver on his promise to reignite his country's passion for Davis Cup. Not only that, the people of Zimbabwe were promised the kind of sporting theatrical that would inspire their team to heroic heights.

The T-shirts were already at the printers with their colorful, intimidating message: "Sampras and Agassi, welcome to the Sound and the Fury." But only Agassi would be there to see it.

After the pair crossed searing paths in the semifinals of the Australian Open—a match in which Sampras came within two points of victory in a fourth-set tiebreak, then succumbed to Agassi's brilliance in the fifth—Sampras revealed that he had damaged a hip flexor right at the start. He would need a night's rest and a doctor's examination the next morning to determine whether he could travel to Harare.

Sampras duly came to a press conference and announced he was unfit. A question about whether he would have defaulted the Australian Final had he beaten Agassi was greeted with a withering look. "A hypothetical situation," he answered. But was it really?

Sampras had telephoned the captain the previous evening, catching McEnroe—who had been warned of the possibility of his withdrawal—as he dined at home with his family. Their conversation was brief but as McEnroe had said presciently, "I didn't think Pete wanted to come to Zimbabwe in the first place."

To make matters worse, the always reliable Martin had gone down with a viral infection. Possible alternatives went racing through McEnroe's gray matter. Jim Courier, a most noble Davis Cup warrior who still thirsted for combat, was not at this moment in the best frame of mind. Since he had not been selected for the squad, he had already booked a ski vacation. What about Vince Spadea? Three first-round defeats suggested a man unsuited to the unique demands of the competition.

Next in line was Chris Woodruff. The twenty-seven-year-old from Knoxville had only just returned home after a strenuous Australian Open, in which he had reached the quarterfinals before falling to Sampras.

But a call from the Davis Cup Captain was manna from heaven. "This, for me, is single-handedly the biggest honor in my career, no doubt about it," said the man from Tennessee, hardly daring to speculate on how sweet the honor would be.

And so, the disparate elements of the U.S. team arrived in Harare to be greeted by a Zimbabwe squad of which the bedrock was once more the Black brothers, Byron and Wayne. "The most famous sporting Blacks in Zimbabwe are two whites," said Paul Chingoka, the genial president of Tennis Zimbabwe.

What these remarkable brothers, their sister Cara, and their father Don, who was to die so young later in the year, had achieved for tennis in their country was beyond parallel. The family had given their sport a meaning, a vitality that was evident the moment the U.S. team arrived for the banquet the evening before the tie began and was to be endorsed throughout its three momentous days. The Blacks loved every minute of the pre-event gathering. They were in their element—relaxed yet focused, low-key yet determined. Their dark eyes blazed with eagerness. In contrast, the body language of the Americans oozed disenchantment. They would rather have been spared the group of musicians fronted by a singer who maintained one monotonous dirge for a full fifteen minutes. The hotel banquet room was packed and stiflingly hot, the queues for the food were inordinate, and the American table disappeared beneath a welter of flash bulbs and autograph hunters. Andre Agassi looked peeved, but, like the sensitive soul he is, rose to his feet to make a speech about playing tennis and especially playing tennis in Zimbabwe that brought the house down. Another country had been conquered. They loved Agassi for his charm and dignity. They loved McEnroe, too. No one could wait for the match to get started.

What would McEnroe make of the Harare City Sports Centre, a tumbledown venue ten minutes from the central sprawl of the capital? During the tie against Australia in 1999, a thunderstorm broke overhead and water dripped onto the court through the tinny structure overhead. During Thursday's practice the same thing happened and so, as Friday dawned and the clouds gathered, the Zimbabweans sent workers onto the roof to hammer down the ramparts.

The draw for the tie had taken place in a huge marquee in the front garden of Comrade President Robert Mugabe's palatial home. The contrast between the grandeur of the surroundings and the roads outside could not have been more marked—though the unsettling presence of his army guards and their nervous disposition spoke volumes of the unrest of the nation as a whole.

Zimbabwe was a country on the verge of civil unrest. The queues for petrol stretched miles, a few indiscreet blacks talked of their hatred of the president, and the whites, especially those in rural areas, were living on a nervous edge. But whatever was happening in the townships and villages outside the gates of his fortress, Mugabe was not going to let anyone think he was not in absolute control.

The red carpet trailed from Mugabe's house to the marquee, and as the band struck up, he came into view, strutting peacock-like to his high chair at the head of the table where tennis dignitaries of the U.S. and Zimbabwe were seated. McEnroe hardly seemed to notice he was there. Mugabe talked, with humor, of the "dwarfs against the giants" and the five members of the home team—the Blacks, Kevin Ullyett, Genius Chidzikwe, and Captain Gavin Siney—visibly stiffened.

Agassi, no leviathan himself, paid due respect to the competition he was about to enter for the first time since a much-publicized falling out with the United States Tennis Association over its decision to drop the eminent Dr. George Fareed, now reinstated, from its entourage.

"This is a fantastic event, but so much of it is about enjoying being around the people you're around," said Agassi, who had played nineteen ties in twelve years since his debut against Peru in 1988. "There's pressure, a lot of expectation, and there's going to be a great feeling if we can accomplish this weekend. I think my body has adjusted to the altitude, but there's going to be a lot of running around to be done.

"Once I was on the team, I was on the team—no doubt about it. It is always an incredible challenge. Anything can happen in the Davis Cup. Playing either Wayne or Byron in the opening rounds of a Grand Slam is totally different to what we can expect here. I've given much of my career to this competition, and if you have an organization that allows a team to feel like a team then it's a great addition to your life any time it comes along."

Agassi would play Wayne Black in the opening rubber, with Woodruff to follow against Byron. Three days to become accustomed to the conditions had not dimmed Agassi's intent. "The greatest thing about tennis is that two people have to deal with the same circumstances," he said. "The one thing I pride myself on is that if somebody else can do it, then so can I. If things go smooth, I'll feel good about it; if things are difficult, I'll adjust. It's as simple as that."

There was little adjustment required. The younger Black, who'd led Sampras two sets to love in the third round in Melbourne, threatened extensively, holding the first break points of the tie in the fifth game that Agassi had to lunge and dart across court to save. The drumbeats quickened. And there was certain consternation about the call on set point when the American appeared to have driven a backhand service return an inch too far before Black's subsequent half-volley was called long.

On such intricacies can these ties be determined. Agassi went on to win 7–5, 6–3, 7–5, fulfilling the first part of the requirement America had placed on him: to make sure of a point from each of his singles matches.

"I didn't have a chance to get derailed from my focus today because I was worried about Wayne and that's when you know everything's in the right place out there," said Agassi. "It helps that there's somebody out there who's been in this environment a number of times. John's well aware of what's required to raise your level. At this stage of my career, I'm not having a problem staying focused. But if it was possible to get off track at all, he's ideal to keep you on. He was saying all the right things out there. He knew when I needed to maintain. He knew when to tell me, 'OK, step it up and hit your shots, let him feel you in a couple of different ways here.' He's well aware of your opponent and how he's feeling. It's nice to know he's there."

An incentive for Agassi must have seemed like a millstone for Woodruff. Imagine walking out for your debut for the United States in a strange land with about fifty friends in your corner, 3,950 people rooting for your opponent, nobody giving you a chance, and John McEnroe, that greatest of Davis Cup exponents, rattling into your ear. It is a wonder Woodruff's legs didn't seize up.

To be fair to the guy, Woodruff traded Byron Black blow for blow without a sign of nerves. A first-set tiebreak was required to separate the two men, and it was here that Black pounced and Woodruff's lack of experience in the circumstances conspired to defeat him. One sensed that Woodruff had to win the breaker to have a chance of taking the match, but Byron was too strong, too redoubtable. The thirty-year-old, 5'10" pro, who was raised less than ten miles from the City Sports Center, triumphed 7–6, 6–3, 6–2 to ecstatic Zimbabwean acclaim.

"I've been preparing for this match mentally for three, four months now, since the draw was made," Black said. "It's one of the biggest sporting events in the country, maybe that we'll ever have. I just wanted to give it everything today. I feel sorry for him because it's tough. I've been on the receiving end myself in Morocco and I didn't handle it very well. I know what he's going through."

So the opening day had finished as most neutrals had expected at 1–1. For once, more eyes were focused on Captain Siney than Captain McEnroe. The question, of course, was would Siney choose to alter his initial doubles selection of Wayne Black and Ullyett and play Byron with his brother? After all, a doubles victory was imperative for the home side. With Agassi fired up for the opening reverse singles against Byron, Siney decided to stick with his chosen team.

An hour after play had ended McEnroe sat in the American dressing room, twiddling with his racket and ruminating on the day's play. "I didn't rise to the occasion," he insisted. "I know I'm not out there playing but I believe a good coach can make the difference between winning and losing. I know in my heart I could have done better for Chris.

"That is my attitude. It's one thing if you have Agassi and Sampras. But I've been hired to get results for the USTA and it could be a short tenure if you can't figure out what's best for the players. Unusually for me, I found it difficult to communicate with the players—this noise thing. Maybe I should check the rules to see if I can walk back to the baseline with them.

"You just get so used to being on the court. I don't want to be yelling at the umpire. I don't want to bore everyone. This is why I have to go through it. I know I did a poor job, but that doesn't mean I can't do a better job tomorrow.

"I didn't have anything preordained to say to the team. It's pretty natural. I'm not here to make 'this one for the Gipper' speeches. It's not in my nature to state the obvious. I prefer a more subtle approach. The guys are looking to me for strong leadership and I have to embrace that. Maybe tomorrow it's going to happen for me a little easier. Instead of being an advantage so far, I've been a disadvantage."

It was incredible to sit there and listen to the man. One hoped he would prove to be more inspirational to his team back at base, but this was McEnroe in full spleen-venting mood. He didn't like himself at this critical moment. He was in captaincy denial and he knew he had to come good in forty-eight hours or the worst possible start to his new career was eminently possible.

The doubles, as so often before, was looked upon as the pivotal match. Rick Leach, fresh from his Australian Open success with Ellis Ferreira, was paired with O'Brien; the younger Black with Ullyett as prescribed. Leach had thought his Davis Cup career had ended in 1997 when he was beaten along with Jonathan Stark by the Dutch pair Jacco Eltingh and Paul Haarhuis in California. But here he was back, at age 35, representing the USA.

McEnroe always preferred a left-right combination, so giving Leach the nod ahead of Jared Palmer was no surprise. It was Ullyett's first "live" Davis Cup appearance, and thus, it was to this balding twenty-seven-year-old that the Americans looked for a sign of weakness. Leach, O'Brien, and Wayne Black were Cup-tough. McEnroe was on the edge of his seat.

Ullyett didn't manage to get a first serve into court in his opening service game, Leach survived the first break points, O'Brien was a tower of purpose, Black oozed confidence, and thus, a tiebreak ensued. The Zimbabweans prevailed, 7–4. Looking at McEnroe, it seemed just as well those workmen nailed down the roof so firmly. Was the event going to be McTantrum free? Surely not.

The Zimbabweans had two points at 5–4 on O'Brien's serve to lead two sets to love. Ullyett sent in a backhand service return a foot long; Black missed with a forehand sitter. True to the way these situations so often work out, Black immediately sacrificed his serve but not before McEnroe stood to argue the toss at 15–all with French umpire, Bruno Rebeuh. The debate took so long to resolve at this critical stage of the tie that the Zimbabweans became incensed. Captain Siney rose as if to exchange words with McEnroe.

At the changeover, Swedish referee Stefan Fransson approached McEnroe as he knelt at his team's feet and obviously received a few ill-chosen words in return.

Fransson tapped the umpire's knee. "Captain's warning, United States," intoned Rebeuh. Spectators wondered when was the last time that an American captain—indeed, any captain—had been so rebuked.

The tie was on a knife-edge, and so were everyone's emotions. Leach and O'Brien pocketed the second set then cruised through the third, 6–0. The Zimbabweans regrouped once again, taking the fourth set 7–5 with a single break in the twelfth game on Leach's serve. In the decider, Leach survived a couple of break points in the eighth game with a couple of aces before his serve was threatened once more in the critical twelfth.

The Americans led 40–15, but Ullyett came up with a glorious backhand service return winner and Leach plunked a backhand volley into the net. Deuce. Ullyett's forehand service return winner gave the home side match point. Leach, incredibly, double-faulted. Game, set, match, Zimbabwe.

Joyous echoes were still pulsating around the court. But McEnroe saw it only as some kind of "anti-me" conspiracy. "These guys have to overcome the fact that people are making up for lost time with me," he said. "That's how I feel. I feel bad that my teammates have to deal with that. They have nothing to hang their heads about."

So dawned, hot and cloudy, the reverse singles day. The likely scenario was for Agassi to win against Byron Black, and Woodruff pitched into what would be the most awesome appointment of his tennis career against Wayne Black.

But who can ever demand in tennis? Agassi had to be a clear favorite—he had come to Zimbabwe for the precise reason to lead his country to success—but it meant little in the vicarious world he inhabited. He had to deliver, but could he survive? I was the only British journalist to witness the full extent of the extraordinary events in Harare, and my words in the *Daily Telegraph* tell the story as the drama finally unfolded.

Andre Agassi has lived and thrived in the spotlight for all of his sporting life. Yesterday Chris Woodruff learned for the first time in seven obscure years as a professional what it is to be defeated by his fellow man.

The first time anyone took any notice of Woodruff was at Roland Garros four years ago when he defeated Agassi in the second round. As they walked to the court before the match, Agassi decided to introduce himself. "How are you doing? My name's Andre," he said. "As if I didn't know," a startled Woodruff replied. We know both of them now.

Together yesterday, these two distinctly different Americans performed in the heroic traditions of the Davis Cup to secure their country a place in the second round of the World Group. On completing a straight-set victory over Byron Black, the world number 1, suffering from the effects of the heat, humidity and breath-constricting altitude, vomited in the ball-container behind the umpire's chair and had to return to the hotel to rest. He said he would have carried on into a fourth set if he had needed to, but his complexion betrayed such brazen optimism.

Up had to step Woodruff, who had lost his first singles on Friday to the elder Black. He had watched the doubles team falter on Saturday, stayed in the dressing room during Agassi's match, and had to walk into an arena expecting Wayne Black to put him to the sword. Two hours and fifty-eight minutes later, with his 6–3, 6–7, 6–2, 6–4 victory, Woodruff was up where he had never been before.

Nothing this twenty-seven-year-old from Knoxville, Tennessee, has ever done—or maybe will ever do again—can possibly compare with the elation he felt as his fifteenth and final ace sped past Black's despairing reach. With this thundering crackshot, he tossed his racquet into the air, from where it almost landed on the head of John McEnroe, who was racing from his chair to embrace Woodruff in an all-enveloping bear hug.

He wouldn't have minded. McEnroe's debut in the captain's role he has coveted for years, ended in a quite remarkable victory for Woodruff, the first man to say "yes" to the captain's request for someone to fill the shoes of Pete Sampras for a tie pitted with problems. "Emotions like these are what you dream about," said McEnroe later. "I just want some time to savor the aroma of it. We worked so hard together as a team especially after yesterday when things were looking bleak. And yet we persevered. The plane ride home looks a lot shorter right now.

"Who can ever criticize Andre's character again? He goes down to Australia, wins the title there, flies here, takes three days to get himself together in totally foreign conditions, and he's shown so much heart and character. It says so much for him, for all of these guys. This team will beat the Czech Republic in the next tie, you have my word on that."

McEnroe, warned by the French umpire Bruno Rebeuh for his language at the start of the third set, now has to confront the dilemma of whether to shuffle his pack for the second-round tie against the Czechs, almost certain to be staged at the Los Angeles Forum in April. Sampras, who missed the tie with a hip-flexor injury, should come into consideration, but McEnroe's initial feeling last night was to select the same four players who have provided him with one of the highest peaks of his colorful career.

How could he not select Woodruff? Everything that was asked of him, he gave. When the Zimbabwe press insisted yesterday that "this American meat is ready for roasting," they obviously had the novice in mind. Indeed, the home team had said before the tie that they knew their only chance was to stalk Woodruff until he crumbled. It simply didn't happen; Woodruff played a level of tennis in the first and third that his Davis Cup forefathers would have greatly appreciated.

There was one overriding element of history in the outcome of the tie. It was the first time since 1981 that an American team had come from 2–1 down on the second day to win a Davis Cup tie. The winner that day was a certain JP McEnroe, who defeated Mexico's Raul Ramirez. Arthur Ashe was captaining the U.S. team for the first time. Yesterday was the seventh anniversary of Ashe's untimely death. Maybe this victory was in the stars.

Maybe it truly was. The Americans were up there alongside those stars a couple of hours later, stepping onto the British Airways 747 to begin the long journey back home, via London's Gatwick airport. "This has been some occasion," remarked McEnroe. "Something I will never ever forget. These boys have done their nation proud."

The hopes of Britain rest on the shoulders of Tim Henman.

above Henman's lack of support against the Czechs sealed Britain's fate in the opening round.

previous spread Agassi needed to win two points if the USA was to survive the opener against Zimbabwe. Chris Woodruff, in his first Davis Cup tie, rose to the occasion, winning the fifth and deciding rubber to give USA and new Captain McEnroe a place in the quarterfinals.

OSTRAVA BOUND

Another team up in the air was Britain. In an aircraft privately chartered by the captain, David Lloyd, they returned as defeated troops after losing to the Czech Republic in Ostrava. The Czechs had tossed Jiri Novak into the air after the nation that spawned Navratilova and Lendl had won the tie in Ivan's birthplace. The result had not been exactly unexpected. Once Greg Rusedski was written out of the tie following his Christmas foot surgery, the dearth of talent in Britain behind the Canadian-born leftie and resident flag-bearer Tim Henman was certain to be exposed. It had not helped the cause when, at the Australian Open, Lloyd went on the record criticizing the fitness levels of the second-string British players, Jamie Delgado and Arvind Parmar. It was to be one of the costliest interviews he had ever given. The British Lawn Tennis Association was smarting from a long series of body punches delivered by Lloyd, a self-made multi-millionaire not averse to criticizing those he felt were holding tennis back. Lloyd and the LTA had been at loggerheads for a long time.

During the Ostrava tie, Lloyd had taken one of the more reputable British tennis writers aside and told him he would be leaving his post after the relegation playoff into which Britain had now been plunged. But the LTA—who insisted they knew nothing of Lloyd's future plans—had already decided enough was enough. They would now act to rid themselves of a consistent thorn in their side.

The tie itself had followed predictable lines. In the first singles, Henman trailed Slava Dosedel by two sets to love before staging a fabulous rally, dredging reserves of courage and determination in the face of defeat. Seldom had he played more boldly in such a precarious position. Henman triumphed 6–7, 5–7, 6–1, 7–5, 6–3 in a grueling four hours and twenty-two minutes, disappearing beneath a bear-hug from Lloyd, the man who had first discovered him some fifteen years earlier. Those watching on television at home remarked how Henman seemed cool in Lloyd's company, that he seemed to ignore all that his captain said, that their special relationship might now not have been all it was cracked up to be.

"It's great to have come back from two sets down, but it's only the first rubber of the tie. Nothing to get carried away with," said Britain's number 1.

He was right to be cautious. Delgado had to face Novak, a tall order not just because of the disparity of their heights, but also because he had only represented his country once in Davis Cup, three years earlier, and had lost both singles.

For Britain this would have been the perfect time for Delgado to add a win to his Davis Cup credentials, but Novak was by far the more solid player. Though Delgado hung in valiantly, it was of little surprise when Novak emerged with a 6–4, 7–6, 6–3 victory to level the tie.

Henman had to come back again the following day, this time in partnership with Neil Broad, the South African–born doubles specialist with whom he had collected the silver medal at the 1996 Atlanta Olympics. Richard Evans of the *Sunday Times*, being as polite as he could, described Broad as "being built like an England number 8 forward." For the rest of the world, that means heavy. Broad needed more than just brute force against the splendid combination of Novak and David Rikl and, rarely free of nerves at the start of a match, he required several pep talks from Henman to settle into the rhythm of the contest. It might have been better had Henman been able to handle the racquet for Broad as well.

from left to right Slava Dosedel lost a heartbreaker to Tim Henman before Jiri Novak won both of his singles and the doubles to put the Czech Republic through against Britain.

The defining moment of the match—and thus the tie—came when the Brits had two set points in the opening set. Broad pushed a forehand service return into the net, Novak responded with a clinical volley winner. The Czechs took the first set on a tiebreak and Lloyd found himself in the now-familiar position of being two sets down when Henman produced his eighth double-fault of the match. Though the British side rallied to take the third set, they could not sustain it and at the moment of their 7–6, 6–4, 6–7, 6–2 defeat, Broad announced his Davis Cup retirement. "My wife is expecting another child in July and, anyway, it's time to give the younger guys a chance," he said.

Henman was once again left to shoulder the burden of having to defeat Novak to keep his country's hopes alive. It was an unequal struggle. "We are basically a two-man team and when one of those is injured, we're right up against the wall," said Lloyd, as Henman went down 6–4, 6–2, 6–2 to Novak. The captain was left to consider the prospect of a playoff the week after Wimbledon, but as events transpired, it would not be Lloyd's problem, anyway. He was dismissed two weeks after the tie, the LTA moving with more boldness than usual in dealing with an employee they believed was affecting morale. Almost as an afterthought, John Lloyd, brother and coach, was out as well. David Lloyd threatened legal redress, but the two sides settled before British tennis's dirty linen was splattered across the law courts. Lloyd went back to his private tennis initiatives, with the promise that he would find the next British tennis champion before the LTA did.

SWISS MISS

If it was daggers drawn in Britain, there was not much love lost among the Swiss either. The appointment of the former world top ten player Jakob Hlasek was greeted with a storm of protest. Hlasek may have had the most total wins, the most singles wins, and the most doubles wins for Switzerland in Davis Cup—a record that suggested he was steeped in the fraternal ethos of esprit de corps—yet, by his first team announcement, he had caused the kind of uproar that is not often associated with Swiss sport.

Marc Rosset is not, perhaps, the most popular player in the world among his peers—he is a maverick given to variable moods and melancholia. As Hlasek and Rosset had never seen eye to eye, this was the perfect opportunity for the new captain to redress that situation, and he dropped Rosset from the team.

This opened a festering sore. "I'm going to be here for a long time," said Hlasek. "It's tough, but I want to create a spirit for the future and this is the right time. The behavior of Rosset toward the federation and to me has been completely unacceptable. He's always been a very difficult player to get along with. Either you're on his side or you're not. I've decided not to take him because of the harmony I need in the team. It is a decision taken for human reasons. Also, he's not the player he was."

Hlasek's decision not only irritated Rosset, but it caused an immediate split in the Swiss camp. Roger Federer, the former ITF World Junior Champion, could have seen this as an incredible opportunity to step into the limelight, but he was as irate as Rosset. The eminently likeable George Bastl was similarly predisposed, which left Michael Kratochvil, a newcomer called in by Hlasek for his Davis Cup debut, as the only player who had any rapport with the new captain.

At any other time, a tie against the defending champions was a great opportunity, something to cherish, especially when Mark Philippoussis was once again dangling Tennis Australia on a string about his intentions. With the Swiss in disarray and the Aussies far from happy with the all-too-familiar prevarication from Philippoussis at selection time, it was difficult to predict what would happen.

It wasn't until a week before the team departed for Zurich that John Newcombe, in his last year as Davis Cup captain, and Geoff Pollard, the president of Tennis Australia, could formally announce that their team, without the still-recovering Patrick Rafter, would be Lleyton Hewitt, Sandon Stolle, Wayne Arthurs, and last year's Final's hero, Mark Philippoussis.

Newcombe, in a press conference to announce the squad, went on the attack for a player with whom he had had differences in the past. "I think Mark always said he was keen to play Davis Cup this year, and the speculation from the media was whether he would play in the first match or not. He is playing, so some of you will probably have to go and change your stories now—sorry about that."

There was never any doubting the commitment of Hewitt to the national cause. The eighteen-year-old from South Australia had enjoyed a compelling journey through the first month of the year, winning the titles in Adelaide and Sydney prior to a campaign in the Australian Open en route to the Round of 16—a thirteen-match winning streak.

Asked for his prediction, Captain Newcombe said, "We will have to fight twice as hard to retain the Cup as we had to win it in the first place." Hewitt was heavily favored to defeat Bastl in the opening singles and, after a rocky start, he pulled through 4–6, 6–3, 6–2, 6–4. Now it was Philippoussis's turn.

The Swiss were keen to see how Hlasek and Federer, who had not been short of words on the appointment, got on together. The body language said more than simple words. At every changeover, Federer buried his head into a towel and turned away from his captain. For all intents and purposes, the teenager was out on his own, cutting himself off from help, disengaging from the time-honored tradition of attending to a supportive word in the ear.

It didn't look as if Federer needed any help. Though he had had a fabulous junior career, finishing 1998 as the number 1 in the world and winning the Wimbledon Boys title, the lad from Basel had not yet made a telling breakthrough into the senior ranks, although that breakthrough would come later in the year. Federer was one more who was forced to recognize that a gold-tinged time in the juniors did not necessarily correlate to instant success in the pros.

But Federer excelled in what was the biggest match of his career to date. Whether or not the advice came from Hlasek, Federer decided on a policy of all-out attack and stunned Philippoussis 6–4, 7–6, 4–6, 6–4.

The Swiss could hardly believe their good fortune, which was to be underlined in the doubles, when Federer teamed with Lorenzo Manta, who reached the fourth round of the 1999 Wimbledon, to defeat Wayne Arthurs and Sandon Stolle in four sets.

Australia was now faced with the unpalatable prospect of becoming only the fifth defending champion to lose in the first round the following year. It had been only eight weeks since Nice.

It was to be Hewitt's turn first and maybe, just maybe, the exertions of the doubles had taken a toll on Federer, for he was only able to stay with Hewitt sporadically, losing in four sets. How ironic that the outcome

of the tie should rest on Philippoussis, who had kept everyone, including his own entourage, guessing until the last moment about his availability for the tie. In the Swiss corner was Bastl, who had won the first set against Hewitt on Friday. The full house in Zurich was ecstatic when Bastl took the opening set against Philippoussis in a tiebreak.

But Philippoussis, the hero of the 1999 Davis Cup Final, had learned to live with the unique pressures of Davis Cup tennis, and the big man managed to prevail in five sets that were the finest in sportsmanship and quality—the hallmarks of this competition. "I felt up and down, I never really believed I had won, but this is the great thing about the competition," said Philippoussis. "Your teammates bring you through."

FRENCH FLOP

So the champions survived, but what of the finalists? France had not recovered from their Nice experience and the air was filled with recriminations.

The feeling in the French camp was they had lost because of a disconcerting mood in the week preceding the Final, when the Aussies bonded and the French unglued. The French number 1, Cedric Pioline, still distraught at losing to Philippoussis in the decisive singles, was involved in lengthy, strident debates with Captain Guy Forget as to the constitution of the 2000 side. The result was that only one member of the last French team of 1999 survived to appear in the first outing of 2000—Pioline himself. Out went Fabrice Santoro, considered a bit of a loner, his doubles partner Olivier Delaitre, and Sebastien Grosjean, and in came Jerome Golmard, Nicolas Escude, and Arnaud Clement. But while the team was different, the

result was the same, and France fell to Brazil, whom they had defeated in the previous year's quarterfinals.

As its venue, Brazil had chosen Florianopolis, the home of its favorite son, Gustavo (Guga) Kuerten. What it could not choose were the conditions. It pelted rain the entire practice week, so much so that on the morning of the opening rubber between Pioline and Fernando Meligeni, the court was doused in gasoline and set afire in an attempt to dry the sodden clay.

There was a lingering scent of burning gasoline when Pioline and Fernando Meligeni, the Brazilian number 2, walked out for what was to become a duel and a half. Pioline was suffering badly, constantly having to wipe at his sore, reddening eyes. France would weep with him, for Meligeni prevailed across five sets in three hours and forty-eight minutes for one of the most important victories of his career.

"There was a lot of pressure on us at the start," said Meligeni. "In the days before the match everyone was talking about the 1998 World Cup Final result and that this was the chance for Brazil to have its revenge. You know how much of a soccer country Brazil is. It might have been revenge for the fans and for the press, but we could not go out with revenge in our minds.

"We just had to concentrate on playing a team full of talent, especially Cedric, one of the finest players in the world. It was very tough for both of us—but I knew that I had to win because I felt that Guga was playing so well he would beat Jerome Golmard. I had the chance to have taken a two-set lead, but even though the court was very heavy and Cedric would have preferred it to be faster, he was playing some huge points."

"I feel I am a much stronger player after what I achieved at Roland Garros in 1999," continued Meligeni, who lost to Andrei Medvedev in Paris. "I had good results in my career, but to reach the semifinals at the

French changed my life. I beat Corretja, Mantilla, Rafter, and El Aynaoui on the way to the semis and all of those wins were so good for my motivation and self-belief. I knew that I had become a very tough player to beat."

So Pioline found as Meligeni hung in to win 7–5, 5–7, 4–6, 6–1, 6–4, offering Kuerten the platform to confirm a 2–0 overnight lead by beating Golmard in four sets. Pioline was asked to hold the cause together in the doubles as well, but the Brazilians were not to look the gift-horse in the mouth. Kuerten and Jaime Oncins were imperious at times during their 6–4, 6–4, 6–4 victory that gave their country a place in the quarterfinals. The Brazilian people had the revenge they had wanted, and the tennis players, well, they were simply delirious.

SPAIN'S SUMMIT

In this year of experiment and change, no country took the bull by the horns in such a sweeping manner as Spain. Manuel Santana may well have changed the landscape in the mid-sixties with his three Grand Slam successes, but defeat at home to Brazil in the first round of 1999 condemned his captaincy.

The Spanish Federation decided that rather than nominate a single captain, they would appoint a technical committee of four of the best brains in the country to select the side: Javier Duarte, Alex Corretja's coach; Jose Perlas, who worked with Carlos Moya and Albert Costa; Jordi Vilaro (Felix Mantilla); and Juan Avendano, the national coach at the Federation. It looked as though it might spawn a thousand late-night arguments, what with the coaches likely to put forward the cases of their own players at the risk of the harmony and

left The year 2000 would be a great one for Brazil's Gustavo Kuerten.

above Brazil's first round victory over France would propel them to the semifinals, while Kuerten, here with Jaime Oncins, would win Roland Garros, the Tennis Masters Cup, and be crowned the new world number 1.

spirit they were charged with raising. "It was a very difficult time for us," said Corretja. "Manolo was our captain and the press thought we kicked him out, but all we had done was to say to the Federation that we would prefer to have our own coaches and they took the decision to relieve Manolo of the captaincy. We all felt we were now involved: the players, coaches, physical trainers, the crowd. The atmosphere was brilliant—we had now a great team spirit."

But with the potential for unrest and disquiet, it was just as well that Spain had drawn the Italians, a team that, despite its arrival in the 1998 Final against Sweden, had fallen on perilous times.

For the first time in the tournament's seventy-year history, there would be no Italian man in the second round at the Foro Italico—a thoroughly depressing statistic. So were those from Murcía, where the Italians were well defeated in two days. Paolo Bertolucci, the Italian captain, was out there on his own against four minds, if only Duarte's body.

Costa had beaten Davide Sanguinetti within a couple of hours in straight sets before Corretja, desperate to put his humiliation by Lleyton Hewitt in Melbourne behind him, faced Andrea Gaudenzi, now back on track after his shoulder surgery. Corretja's return to his favored clay had the desired effect: a four-set victory that gave Spain the kind of advantage they were not to squander.

Though the Italians named Gaudenzi and Diego Nargiso, a team that had won five of their seven Davis Cup doubles and were instrumental in pointing their country toward its 1998 final appearance, they were swamped by Corretja and Juan Balcells in straight sets. Spain eventually won the tie 4–1 and would now face the Russians—a totally different kettle of *pescados*.

from left to right Italians Diego Nargiso and Andrea Gaudenzi suffered a straight sets defeat, as the Spanish went on to celebrate a 4–1 victory in Murcia. Yevgeny Kafelnikov led Russia to a 4–1 triumph over Belgium in Moscow.

RUSSIAN RENAISSANCE

On their return to Moscow for the first round tie against the Belgians, all in the Russian *dacha* was far from rosy. Who knew what mood Yevgeny Kafelnikov would be in after his defeat in the Australian Open final to Agassi? More, there had to be concern about Marat Safin, who not only lost in the opening round in Melbourne to qualifier Grant Stafford, but was fined by the championship for what amounted to failing to give his best.

Belgium, meanwhile, had had a remarkable year in 1999, reaching the semifinals before losing to France. Their captain, Gabriel Gonzales, retained hopes of a similar story, what with Filip Dewulf's health restored and the raw promise of Christophe and Olivier Rochus.

Dewulf, a semifinalist in the French Open in 1997 and once ranked in the top 40, was now earning a living from the scraps of the Challenger circuit as a means of getting back toward his former level of respectability. He came out of the blocks energetically against Kafelnikov and pushed the Australian Open champion for all he was worth through four sets. When his victory was assured, Kafelnikov cited the long journey home and fatigue as excuses for his lack of luster.

Safin had no such problems. Christophe Rochus was enough of a handful: he'd reached the last sixteen in Melbourne before losing, ironically, to Kafelnikov. But the younger Russian held himself together to proclaim, "I didn't know what to expect but I'm so proud and so happy that I could do this for my team and my country." Safin was so full of latent energy that he combined with Andrei Cherkasov for a doubles victory over the Rochus brothers to cement Russia's place in the second round.

from left to right Sjeng Schalken
played number one singles for the
Netherlands in the absence of
Richard Krajicek. Tommy Haas
enjoyed the adulation of the home
crowd by securing victory over the
Dutch.

MECIR'S MERRY MEN

Russia were to be joined there by the Slovak Republic, a team bolstered by the captaincy of Miloslav Mecir, his protégé Karol Kucera, and young Dominik Hrbaty, who had reached the semifinals of Roland Garros the previous year and might have gone to the final had not a long rain shower on that Friday evening interrupted his stirring fight-back against Andre Agassi.

For Kucera, having Mecir both as a personal and Davis Cup coach was something to cherish. "Nobody knows my game better," he said, "and it is true to say he can tell whether I am in the right shape to play or not in Davis Cup. We don't go into long conversations about it. He knows."

Mecir couldn't have known his country would start the year in such devastating form. The Austrian captain, Gunther Bresnik, declared that his side had little chance—just how little was emphasized within twenty-four hours. Kucera and Hrbaty sliced through Markus Hipfl and Stefan Koubek in straight sets (a failure of the stadium lights in the Hrbaty match couldn't mask the severity of the pounding). But Austrian pain did not end there, as the Slovak pair combined to defeat Julian Knowle and Alexander Peya in straight sets in the doubles.

"We were ready for a fight, but I was delighted with the manner of our victory," said Mecir, as lugubrious off-court as he was on it in his playing pomp. "If Karol and Dominik can maintain their form, we should fear no one."

PINBALL WIZARD

German tennis was in need of a similar strain of self-belief. The Becker era had come to an end. No longer could, nor should, they have to rely on the aura of one man—however supremely talented—to guide them to glory. Nicolas Kiefer's dislike of Becker didn't help, nor did the German media ambivalence toward the goatee-bearded, right-hander on whom his nation's hopes so critically depended.

Kiefer was nowhere to be seen when Captain Carl-Uwe Steeb announced his team to face the Netherlands in Leipzig. Germany hadn't been in the second round of the World Group in a couple of years and that was not an acceptable return. It was up to Tommy Haas, with a 7–1 record in Davis Cup singles, to spearhead his country's challenge. He did not let them down.

The loss of Richard Krajicek was obviously a terrible blow to the Dutch side, but the big man's knees were still giving him trouble. Thus, the equally tall John van Lottum was drawn out of the hat first to play Haas, and though he won the opening set, a tiebreak in the second went the German's way and the rest was something of a cruise. Strangely, the second singles was to follow the same pattern, but this time it fell in Holland's favor. Rainer Schuttler won the first set, but Sjeng Schalken took the second on a tiebreak and swept his opponent aside.

The German Olympic 1996 bronze-medal pairing of Marc-Kevin Goellner—who served better than he could ever remember under such pressure—and David Prinosil beat Paul Haarhuis and Jan Siemerink, which set the stage for Haas to demonstrate the form that took him into the world's top ten in late September 1999. His comprehensive straight-set victory over Schalken led to delirious celebration.

Boris was past history, Nicolas was forgotten, and Tommy, who later in 2000 would win the Olympic silver medal for Germany, was the new hero.

CHRIS WOODRUFF

profile *Chris Woodruff* | **birthplace** *Knoxville, Tennessee* | **birthdate** 1•2•73 | **turned professional** 1993 |

Davis Cup records *singles* 1–1 • *doubles* 0–0

"I'M A SQUIRREL TRYING TO GET A NUT, THAT'S ALL."

Had he not chosen tennis as his profession, Chris Woodruff might have been an extra in American war movies—the squaddie with the short-back-and-sides, who instinctively barks "Yes, sir" and "No, sir" when the company lieutenant bawls him out.

His style on court is that of a military man: stiff-backed, holding his body straight as he marches back to the baseline. There is nothing free-flowing about Woodruff, but what he lacks in aesthetic flair, he more than compensates for in sheer determination. His courage in Harare bore vivid illustration of this.

The twenty-seven-year-old from Tennessee manages to hide his extraordinary passion for tennis behind a well-mannered, if somewhat detached, exterior. His "speak only when spoken to" tendency was obviously part of his upbringing—his mother, Dorothy, is an elementary school teacher. But don't be fooled. Anyone who can step into the Davis Cup as Woodruff did this year and excel is no shrinking violet.

Woodruff's best season was in 1997, when he finished ranked 30 in the world before undergoing a double hernia operation. Then he sprained his left knee while joking around kicking footballs and returned to competitive tennis too soon after arthroscopic surgery.

"I started to worry I'd never play tennis again," Woodruff said. He was off court for six months, during which time his ranking dropped more than 1,300 places. He spent much of that time on the golf course, which was exactly where he was expecting to spend the first two weeks of February, until a certain Mr. McEnroe got in touch.

Having won two deciding fifth rubbers in his illustrious career, Jim Courier knows a bit about the energy of Davis Cup ties, and as the decisive match against Wayne Black drew close, he muttered aloud how Woodruff might cope, having lost to Byron Black comprehensively on the opening day.

"If I were betting, I wouldn't have any money on Chris—not under those circumstances, not after the way the first match went," Courier said. Todd Martin, who would become Woodruff's doubles partner in the semifinal

later in the year, called his friend on the phone the night before he played Black to offer words of encouragement but wondered if they would have any impact.

"I was definitely a little overwhelmed by the situation," Woodruff recalls. "Here I was, a guy who hadn't really made it big in tennis, not really big, given this chance to play a crucial role for my country. How did I know how I'd react? But I knew you could throw everything—rankings, who's the better player—out the window in Davis Cup."

Woodruff went to great lengths to make it to Harare. From the Australian Open—where he defeated Tim Henman in the fourth round only to lose to Pete Sampras in the quarters—Woodruff embarked on a journey from Melbourne to Los Angeles, Cincinnati, Knoxville, Charlotte, New York, and Johannesburg, before landing in the Zimbabwean capital.

His extensive travels made his performance that rainy Sunday afternoon in a stadium far from Tennessee all the more remarkable. He became the first American rookie since Raymond Little in 1906 to win the crucial deciding match. In the world of tennis—in which Woodruff has many admirers—his performance was recognized for its sheer bravery. McEnroe's delirious reaction to his victory (he was hugging him before the umpire had finished reading the score) was one of the great images of sport in 2000.

And Woodruff excelled knowing his limitations. "I don't look at myself as being all that good," he says with refreshing honesty. "I guess I'm better than average. You're not given a book about what to expect on tour, and I was beaten up pretty good early on. My confidence dropped because I couldn't put matches away. But I'm not as hard on myself as I used to be. Put it this way, I'm a squirrel trying to get a nut, that's all."

The accumulation is growing, but not as fast as the player himself would like. "Maybe I haven't entered the zone where I feel like I can win every time I play," he says. "That's the breakthrough I'm waiting for. But I feel like I'm coming into my own."

QUARTERFINAL ROUND

THEY STILL CALL AUSTRALIA HOME

Mark Woodforde headed for Miami International Airport for the twenty-hour haul to Adelaide. Todd Woodbridge got into his car and took the Florida Turnpike to his home in Orlando. The finest doubles team of their generation—some would argue any generation—went their separate ways in the week of the quarterfinal and nothing was designed more vividly to illustrate how critical the ITF's steadfast policy on numbers for team selection had become.

Woodbridge wanted nothing more than to join his partner on the journey to Australia to help drive home the advantage he and Woodforde famously helped secure in the 1999 Final against France at Nice's Palais des Expositions three months earlier. The Woodies had been part of a winning Davis Cup team for the first time, the exhilarating memory burnished inside them, and they were beginning to wonder if it could ever happen again.

Woodforde, remember, said in Nice that he'd decided to retire from international competition, so for him to be considered at all in 2000 was something of a seismic shift in priorities. Australia had not given up hope of persuading him that there was plenty of life back in those ginger-freckled legs. A barbecue held in early March in the back garden of his home in Rancho Mirage, California, to which John Newcombe and Tony Roche were invited, led to a rethink.

"Newk and Rochey sounded me out about the possibility of playing in certain circumstances," said Woodforde. "I was happy to be back as a part of it again, but I guess a part of me only wanted to return if I could play with Todd. But, I also knew I was in no position to dictate, the choice has to be the captain's." Once the Australian captain-coach duo realized Woodforde was open to persuasion, they didn't hesitate.

Woodbridge was left behind to restate his belief that the captains should be allowed to pick five players per team, thus giving a player of his doubles quality a greater chance of selection. As it was, with only four players allowed to be nominated, the captains usually chose one doubles player and had to try to work out which of his three singles players would best knit together come the pivotal rubber on the Saturday afternoon.

As far as Australia was concerned, one of the Woodies was going to be out of favor and Woodbridge was crestfallen to learn he would not be selected. To his credit, he understood why

from left to right Lleyton Hewitt continued his Davis Cup winning ways at home in Adelaide, while David Prinosil played the match of his life but lost to Wayne Arthurs.

previous spread A capacity crowd cheered Spain on to victory in the quarterfinals.

his partner was given the preferential treatment, for at thirty-four years of age, Mark Woodforde was undoubtedly the finest doubles player in the sport of tennis since John McEnroe's gray hairs started to sprout.

But the Woodbridge argument had its merits. "If Newk had his way, I'm sure he'd put us in without a doubt," he said. "With the new rule of being able to substitute the singles player, he can't afford to have what happened a few years back in South Africa when a couple of us got sick and injured and couldn't play. The rules define what he has to try to do. I've offered to try really hard and put forward that we can get an extra member and expand the competition so it allows a double combination to play.

"If you have the best competition in the world, you have to allow for the best team to be able to play in it. Right now, it doesn't allow the best team—us—to play. People say we're trying to change the rule for our benefit, but that won't be the case in 2001 because we'll no longer be together. But it needs to be in place for the future for countries that have a set doubles team. I'm really pushing for that."

The Woodies' statistics backed Woodbridge's case. The pair had just won their fifty-sixth doubles title in the final of the Ericsson Open on the delightful island of Key Biscayne, Florida, with a 6–3, 6–4 victory over the Czech-Slovak partnership of Martin Damm and Dominik Hrbaty. They were thus one victory short of joining two of the giant partnerships: John McEnroe and Peter Fleming of the United States and South Africans Bob Hewitt and Frew McMillan, who collected fifty-seven championships in the Open Era. Few would put it past the Woodies overhauling that record sometime later in the year (indeed, it would turn out to be a glorious 2000, with the French Open title for the first time, Wimbledon for the sixth, and an Olympic final added to their resume).

The Davis Cup didn't count in the statistics, but the thought of playing for Australia together again superceded personal achievement. "There's nothing I can do about it, but it will be hard sitting back knowing what the team is going through and I shall be off at a regular tournament, which I need to do. I'd love to be on that court in Adelaide," said Woodbridge. "This is an event where you have to put everything on the line. You play in a regular tournament and you lose, you feel sorry for yourself. No one else cares. In Davis Cup, you're under extreme pressure and it can make or break players. I've seen it break a lot of people."

One felt for this extremely likeable guy, but Newcombe, in the existing circumstances, knew he could change his singles choice an hour before play on the final day, so it was not as imperative as it once had been to choose two doubles specialists. Thus, for what he knew could be his last tie as captain, Newcombe decided to select Lleyton Hewitt and Wayne Arthurs for the singles, teaming the apparently ageless Woodforde with Pat Rafter in the doubles. No Philippoussis, perhaps, but no great worries either. Oh that German Captain Carl-Uwe Steeb had such a variety of riches at his disposal!

The Germans were terribly understrength. Nicolas Kiefer refused to contemplate a place in the team, even though the man with whom he'd had his bitter quarrels in the past, Boris Becker, was no longer a part of Germany's Davis Cup setup. Kiefer's indignation about Davis Cup, which would be resolved for the 2001 competition, was hard to swallow, but all the persuading in the world—even his Australian coach Bob Brett was suffering from mixed emotions—could not make him change his mind. Tommy Haas, the hero of Leipzig in the opening round, was not available for selection because of a hip injury. Thus Steeb, also denied the services of the highly promising Rainer Schuttler due to a late calf-muscle strain, was forced to rely

for a quarterfinal on grass on two players, Michael Kohlmann and David Prinosil, whose Davis Cup singles pedigrees were, being kind, pretty negligible.

So the opening match was Hewitt, who was already winner of three titles on the ATP Tour and looked as if he prepared for every match on raw steak, against Kohlmann, who stood at 158 on the entry list and was summoned to the squad the previous week from playing doubles in a challenger in Magdeburg. It was no contest, surely. From the moment he heard the German national anthem, Kohlmann's legs had turned to the consistency of sauerkraut. Hewitt gave him a hiding, losing only four games in three sets. If the Adelaide crowd was disappointed not to see him make more of a fight of it, they were to spend the next four hours and thirteen minutes gripped by one of those classic matches the reformers would unstitch from the embroidery of the sport.

On any other day, in most tournaments in the world, Arthurs against Prinosil would be just another result. In Davis Cup, it resonated with meaning and purpose. These two men—who had never known what it was like to be feted as heroes in their home countries, who spent their careers in the middle market of professional tennis, excellent professionals, worthy men, who had been dragged from relative anonymity to the heart of this incredible competition—rose to the sense of the occasion. There were two breaks of serve in the entire marathon: for Prinosil to lead 2–1 in the second set and then, in the last game, as Arthurs became a hero with a 7–6, 3–6, 7–6, 6–7, 11–9 victory on his fourth match point. "I think I was a little bit better than him, but he made the last point," said the German.

Arthurs, with a perfect record in Davis Cup singles after his victories over Yevgeny Kafelnikov and Marat Safin in the 1999 semifinal, said all he did was "hang in there." There was a lot more to it than that, but the

from left to right Pat Rafter and
Lleyton Hewitt watched from court-
side as Wayne Arthurs won a five-set
thriller against David Prinosil.
Michael Kohlmann won only four
games on his debut for Germany
against Hewitt. Woodforde and
Rafter celebrate their five-set victory
over Marc-Kevin Goellner and David
Prinosil to seal Australia's triumph.

laconic Australian left-hander, who is based in Pinner, Middlesex, England, had ignited his home crowd, laying the basis for a weekend of celebration, as Woodforde, reveling in the surroundings, and Rafter held off the staggering fight back from Marc-Kevin Goellner and Prinosil to win 10–8 in the fifth. Woodforde and Rafter embraced. Woodbridge was home in Florida at the time, with a thought gnawing away at him that he would not play Davis Cup ever again. He was deeply sad.

THE PETE AND ANDRE SHOW

Across the North American continent, John McEnroe was in a contemplative mood, with the home tie against the Czech Republic on his Los Angeles doorstep. Andre Agassi had limped away from Key Biscayne on a dodgy right ankle, but Pete Sampras had flowed through the tournament in the pink. The two were certain picks—Chris Woodruff's Harare heroics aside. But could McEnroe be certain that they were both in the mood to play against a relatively undistinguished side, in what was only the second round?

"Andre is going to come over and try to swat a few," the captain said. "He told me not to worry, but that's part of the job. You got to figure these things are going to happen. He's hurting a little bit, but I anticipate, in his case, the energy that he'll get from this will be real positive and will help him."

With a poignancy that made him wish he was still out there on the court, McEnroe recalled that Sampras and Agassi formed, with him and Jim Courier, the team that won the Cup in Switzerland eight years earlier. "I felt quite possibly it was the greatest team that was ever put together by America," he said. "Look at all of our records over the year. It was something special. For me it was a very emotional time. I was going through the beginnings of a divorce. Davis Cup was probably the only event I could have played at that time. I felt like my whole family—my children, friends, the team, the people that came to the match—rallied around. It was quite a memorable match for me. I didn't even know if I could do it. I really wasn't up to playing. I had pulled out of a series of exhibitions and was supposed to play a few events in Europe. But I needed to be there [in the Davis Cup Final] and that was the last match I ever played in Davis Cup, playing with Pete in the doubles. It's gone full circle in the sense that I am now trying to get these guys to really embrace and get behind Davis Cup.

"It's an interesting time. If you look at society in general, people forget. You see people making a million dollars out of nowhere whereas making a million dollars used to have an incredible magic to it. Now they make it sound like it's easy."

Dealing with pampered superstars was one thing, but McEnroe also had to tell the hero of Harare, Chris Woodruff, that he was not going to be selected for the tie. "It was hard. There are not a lot of good parts about the job. You feel bad that you have to tell someone who obviously had the greatest moment of his career, 'Thanks a lot, but keep ready now,' in a sense.

"He's sitting there in Tennessee feeling like he's not part of it. He, in all likelihood, would be the guy I would call once someone couldn't play. It's hard, that part of it. It's not fun at all. Chris struggled with it. I felt like he would because of the emotion of that win. Also, people are paying more attention to him. All of a sudden, they are like, 'Chris Woodruff.' They know who he is quite a bit more and he hasn't handled that well. There is a letdown and you have to dig deep inside yourself to figure out how to get pumped up again. He hasn't found that yet."

He had no such fears for Sampras. The Harare problem had blown over, though there was something undoubtedly playing at the back of the captain's mind concerning absolute trust in the commitment of one of the greatest performers in the world. But the opening night shook the Forum to its very foundations.

First, Agassi didn't come out of the dressing room for the national anthems, a move that the Czechs picked up on and the press seized and turned into a deliberate snub for the visitors. Agassi just said he didn't expect there to be a ceremony before the Friday ties when it usually takes place before the Saturday doubles. McEnroe could have done without these sorts of distractions but the media was happy to seize on any discord and see how the volcanic one would react. They hardly needed to force the issue; the outcome of the opening rubber did the job for them.

Sampras, at a breeze, had break points in the second and third service games but failed to capitalize. When such opportunities begin to slip through your fingers, it is easy to get down on yourself. Sampras, with friends in every corner of the auditorium, was nervous, affected more by the tension of the occasion than he thought he would be. He knew that Novak had stayed with him for five sets in the 1996 U.S. Open on Stadium Court at Flushing Meadows, so nothing could be taken lightly. Break points came and went into double figures. Sampras lost the first set on a tiebreak, 7–1, and when the second was pocketed by the Czech, he could find nothing in reserve.

Novak won 7–6, 6–3, 6–2, leaving Sampras to bemoan: "I just got outplayed, and I haven't said that too often throughout my career. I ran into someone who was in the zone. If I could have converted one of those break points and got the crowd a little more involved . . . but when you're zero for fourteen in break points, that just about says it all. He played the match of his life, but I was out here in front of my home crowd, my family, and my friends so, sure, it's very disappointing. It's been a while where I, as I was telling John on the changeover, I don't know what to do. I'm coming in, I'm trying to stay back. No matter what I'm trying, I didn't have the answers.

"There was a great buzz out there, the crowd was on the verge. John and I were talking about it, they wanted to explode, but I just didn't give them the chances to do that. It's not the start we wanted, but I still like our chances for the weekend, that we can get through this and, fortunately, you know, we've got a strong team and we're good teammates."

For Agassi, it was a role reversal from Zimbabwe. There he had played first, won his match, and could relax just a little. This time, he had to be on top of his game and his opponent, Slava Dosedel, immediately. Agassi was equal to the task, as sharp as Sampras had been blunt, rapaciously accepting the chances that came his way against his slight opponent.

"Davis Cup certainly is a high-energy environment, brings out the best in you and you can't afford to be the slightest bit off," Agassi said. "But it's not about caring. It's not about trying. It's about being fit and ready and fresh and rested, and that's not easy to do in a sport that doesn't have an off-season, and there's a lot of times you're not at your best. You saw me last week beat up after three days in a row in the sun.

It didn't take but a little bit to be off, to really feel embarrassed on the court. You saw it today with Pete—
it doesn't take much. There are big problems. It's the nature of the sport."

McEnroe described Sampras's defeat as "a shocking situation." Once more, he took the blame off his
players and preferred to heap it on himself. "Perhaps I should have expected Novak to play that well.
But I didn't foresee that, and we'll just have to. There was a danger of me actually relaxing a little bit if we
had gotten up 2–love. So that was quickly dispelled. They want to make sure I don't sleep a whole lot."

If the captain was tossing and turning on Friday night, it was nothing compared to his struggle for rest on
Saturday. He selected his first choice doubles pair, Alex O'Brien and Jared Palmer, only for them to succumb
in straight sets to Novak and David Rikl, 7–6, 6–4, 6–4. It appeared as if Novak and Rikl—no mean pair
but hardly used to this rarefied air—knew exactly what O'Brien and Palmer were thinking. The Czechs raised
their levels; the Americans fell beneath theirs. It was yet another reminder to the Americans that world
superiority was not something to be taken for granted.

O'Brien said he didn't believe the United States would be in a situation like this. It was both naive and
arrogant to expect to be 3–0 ahead, but "that's why it's a different game, a different animal," he said.
"I'd say we're a little stunned to be in this situation. But, you know, we've got two great players and I'm
excited to have these guys out on the court playing for me tomorrow and our country."

For the first time since he became captain, McEnroe turned on his players just a little. "We're acting like
spoiled kids basically. You have to work harder. We just can't expect to win no matter who you play. We expect
it to happen without having to work for it. Like rich—like my kids, actually. They expect, you know, just hand

left Andre Agassi completes the U.S. comeback victory, following his straight sets defeat of Slava Dosedel.

above Captain John McEnroe applauds from the sidelines.

over the goods, without, you know, putting in the hard work and appreciation of real effort. I think there's extra effort that needs to be taken now. I think that if we're guilty of anything, it's that we haven't worked hard and played hard enough."

Agassi and Sampras had to return to the plate on Sunday and do their stuff with McEnroe's words ringing in their ears. This was the moment to show the world they cared for the Davis Cup—that it still held something dear to them. Novak, having taken so much out of himself against Sampras, was no match for Agassi, losing in straight sets. When Sampras returned to the court, there was to be no repeat of his forlorn display against Novak. Though Dosedel hung in gamely, and, indeed, often threatened to let loose the worst American nightmare, he couldn't stay quite close enough to Sampras, who prevailed 6–4, 6–4, 7–6. The emphasis, once more, was on the captain. Agassi offered this fascinating tidbit when it was pointed out to him that McEnroe seemed to suffer from compulsive nervous energy. "I don't think he struggles to sit still. I think he chooses not to. God bless him for it. I like the energy, you need to have it out there. There's only so much we can do in that arena, but that kind of enthusiasm and support can keep the level of tennis at such a great level, and I feel like that's what it does. When I'm up 4–1 in the third, I'm on the sidelines and I'm feeling like I want to break this guy again. I'm not thinking about closing out the match. I'm thinking about winning every point. It's that kind of enthusiasm that really is offered by the energy of John and by the energy of your team."

Obviously, nothing was going to come easy for McEnroe in this pivotal year. Even in Los Angeles he wasn't bulletproof, so how would the Americans fare in the semifinals, when they would be in a part of the world they had only read about in storybooks?

ALEX'S ARMY CONQUERS RUSSIA

Not only had Spain decided on team choice by committee, but they were happy to spread the message of the competition to every pleasant, sun-soaked corner of the nation. After Murcía staged the first round against Italy, the Federation decided they would host the Russians in Màlaga, a holiday destination and now permanent home to so many British fed up with the terminally soggy grip of their own climate.

Duarte was in the captain's chair again, but the committee had decided upon a change in their singles lineup, ushering in Juan Carlos Ferrero—he of the blond hair, brown eyes, purple racquet strings, and blue-blooded name—for his Davis Cup debut. Ferrero had burst into full public awareness in 1999, winning his first title on the ATP Tour in a converted bullring in Mallorca, where he defeated a chastened Alex Corretja in the final. Now the two of them were to play on the same team.

"We had won quite easily against Italy," recalled Corretja. "But we had expected Russia to give us a much more difficult time. I got the sense that we were so up for the match and they didn't really believe in themselves. We had all the emotions on our side of the net. And, of course, the people were all for us."

Corretja got his side off to a convincing start, defeating Marat Safin, who, like Rip Van Winkle, had yet to rouse himself from the long period of self-defeating slumber. Safin's mood of exasperation with himself and—it appeared—everyone else in the world meant he was fodder for Corretja, who simply ground him into the dust of Màlaga. The scene was thus set for the young prince with the Prince racket, Ferrero, to produce one of the most remarkable opening performances in the history of the competition.

from left to right Alex Corretja leads the Spanish on-court celebrations after winning their Davis Cup quarterfinal against Russia.

"Juan Carlos was just unbelievable," Corretja said. "He is going to be the new star in our country and across the world. It is not just because he is a great player but he is also such a nice guy." Ferrero might have been daunted by the prospect of facing the former world number 1, Yevgeny Kafelnikov, but if he was, he didn't show it. "I slept very well the night before," he said. "I remembered what Alex had said to me, that I didn't have to prove anything to anybody, just to go out there and play my game."

Ferrero won the rubber 6–2, 6–2, 6–2, with a disdain the likes of which marked him down as a precious commodity in a sport looking for new heroes. If Kafelnikov has never taken long to get down on himself in a match, the manner of Ferrero's victory heralded the dawn of a new superstar.

"When the match was over, I shook his hand and said to him, 'Good match,' like I always do when I play, win or lose," said Ferrero. "Kafelnikov looked me in the eye, but didn't say anything back to me." Kafelnikov's demeanor raised once again the deep and abiding questions about the level of his commitment. Here is a player of enormous inconsistency. One day he is the best player in the world, the next a man who has the world's woes on his shoulders.

There was not a glimmer of good sportsmanship after this defeat; indeed, Kafelnikov, fluent in English, refused all attempts by the onsite communications staff to get him to answer questions in press conferences in anything other than his native Russian. Safin, who speaks both Spanish and English, obviously did not want to upset his compatriot and stupidly followed suit. It wasn't a great day for Russia, on or off the court.

They managed to recover some of their poise in the doubles, Kafelnikov and Safin defeating Juan Balcells and Corretja in four sets. It was here that Duarte, Corretja's longtime coach, made a telling move. Knowing

his man was listless and might falter in the opening singles on the third day, he decided to omit him in favor of a refreshed and ready Albert Costa. As it turned out, Corretja might have won it on one leg, for Kafelnikov was in white-flag mood, winning only three games in three sets against Costa for his worst-ever performance in a Davis Cup match. Spain celebrated its place in the semifinals, but Kafelnikov perhaps should have been financially penalized for his attitude throughout the whole tie. Not, of course, that he would have cared.

COPACABANA COMEBACK

So it was to be Spain versus USA on clay; Australia versus whom on grass? Obviously, Brazil was firmly favored, what with home advantage against the Slovak Republic in Rio and Guga Kuerten's performance in reaching the final at Miami where he lost to Sampras in five enthralling sets. But the Slovaks were not to be taken lightly. Before they knew it, Brazil was 1–0 down.

Hrbaty, one of the most improved performers on the tour, comprehensively defeated Fernando Meligeni (like his opponent, a 1999 French Open semifinalist) in straight sets. Meligeni remembers it as a humbling experience. "Dominik was completely unbelievable that day. I tried to hit the ball too high, too slow, harder, to serve and volley, but everything I tried, he was on fire all the time. It was a very tough situation for me to handle because there were ten thousand people in the stadium. Rio is a huge city, where sports mean so much. I reached the semifinals of a Grand Slam and okay, to lose it was sad, but after a while you are happy

again because you have had an incredible two weeks and you say to yourself, 'Okay, I lost. Finish. Remember all the good things you did.' But Davis Cup you lose and, Jesus, it means so much to your country, to everybody. And the people of Brazil, they don't just clap their hands, say congratulations, good match—it comes from the heart. It was tough going back to the hotel and thinking that they were all looking at me."

It was not looking too rosy for Kuerten at two sets to one and 4–2 down in the fourth to Karol Kucera, when something quite remarkable came over the curly mopped Brazilian. That Kucera won only two more games from that moment was testament both to Kuerten's magical talents and the effect the crowd had on its idol.

Kuerten managed to raise himself the next day, teaming with Jaime Oncins to defeat Hrbaty and Kucera in the doubles, but he told Meligeni in the dressing room later that he didn't think he could lift himself again against Hrbaty in the fourth rubber and that his partner should prepare himself to take full responsibility in the fifth. How would Meligeni raise himself from the lows of Friday? What happened to him spoke to the heart of the competition.

"Guga and I have always had a very good relationship," said Meligeni. "He spoke to me on the Saturday night and said he was feeling exhausted, he had cramps in the locker room, and he said it will probably be 2–2. We hoped not, but we could not avoid it. So, I knew I had to win. This is where the team came in. I had to believe in myself and in my tennis. But I needed other people to believe in me also. We had Alex Stober,

the trainer who works on the ATP Tour, and also our third Brazil coach, Joao Zwetch, who was brilliant at getting into my mind. Everyone was saying, 'You're going to win. Okay, let's go.' I looked across at the box and there were ten faces, all urging me to do well. You are bigger than you ever felt in your life—you are like Rambo. And I had a lot of problems in the match. Karol was still playing great tennis; he led by a set and 5–3. I looked across and there was no one looking as if they felt, 'Oh my God, he's not going to do it.' Everywhere was optimism and support."

So much so that Meligeni began to play superhuman tennis, repairing his position and finally wearing Kucera down to the tune of a 5–7, 7–6, 6–2, 6–4 victory to assure Brazil of a place in the semifinals for the first time in eight years.

"I was considered the hero but that is really s***," he said. "There are ten thousand heroes in the stadium, more heroes in your team, and they all help you. I never said at one time that I won the match. We won the match together, all of us."

It was the abiding hymn of the Davis Cup.

ALBERT COSTA

"I BELIEVE I AM A GOOD FIGHTER."

He is Alex Corretja without the perma-smile; Juan Carlos Ferrero without the dashing good looks. But no one in his right mind who studies the formbook would have underestimated the impact Albert Costa was destined to have on the Spanish effort to land the Davis Cup for the first time.

Costa is the guy we have watched countless times across the world, but whose game never left much of a distinctive impression. Indeed, his first name is so often printed in the world's newspapers as Alberto—the Spanish rather than the Catalan spelling—that he has probably suffered from an identity crisis himself.

At most Davis Cup conferences, the questions are asked of Corretja, then the captain, and a cursory one is tossed Costa's way, so as not to embarrass him totally. Yet, when the chips were down as the year wore on, it was increasingly to Costa that Spain's technical selection committee looked to shoulder the most crucial ties. They knew something about him that we had overlooked.

"I prefer it that there are four people who make the decisions because one man might not like me but I have a chance when there are more people debating it," he says. Costa knows that there are other players in the Spanish team of which more is known—and that suits him.

The fact that he had more wins on clay (thirty) than anyone in 1999 is hardly the stuff of riveting conversation over the dinner table. The first note in the ATP Tour's personal information on Albert Costa is that he is no relation to Carlos Costa.

Hewn on the red clay of Catalonia, his tennis game is not the sort to set the pulses racing. It is executed with a minimum of fuss or elaboration but borne of extreme courage and self-belief. He moves smoothly, strikes the ball one handed on the backhand, exerts powerful top spin, and stretches and slides expertly.

"I know I am not famous like other players," he says, "but everyone in the ATP knows I have finished inside the top 20 since 1996 and recognizes how hard that is.

They know I am a very good player, especially on clay, and though I may have slipped a little right now, I think next year maybe will be my best year. But perhaps fame is better suited to other people.

"I am a calm guy, very relaxed, who likes quiet time with his family and his girlfriend, but on the court I become much more aggressive and expressive about myself. I believe I am a good fighter."

And so he has proved. From the moment he was named Newcomer of the Year in 1994 at the age of nineteen, Costa promised to be a little bit more than the ranks of very talented but relatively underachieving Spaniards who flocked the clay courts but didn't have much to offer elsewhere.

Indeed, until the 1999 Masters Series event in Stuttgart, where he defeated Hicham Arazi in the first round, he had lost his previous eighteen career matches indoors—something even he had no answer for. "It had to be something in my head," he said, "because I am no different as a player. It had begun to worry me a lot, not winning an indoor match. Then the next week, I beat Magnus Norman and Greg Rusedski in Paris, so I had proved to myself that this was not a fluke."

In the year 2000, he captured headlines in Britain for the first time, joining his team-mate Corretja in a two-man boycott of Wimbledon over the unfairness of the All England Club's decision to rank players on their grass-court talents rather than their form across a calendar year.

"We felt we had to stand up for ourselves," said Costa, "and I believe the decision made us stronger as people—and helped us in the Davis Cup when people wondered if we had the character to win tough matches."

Those words were to prove a profound adjunct to Spain's progress—and indeed Costa's performance in a pivotal match against Yevgeny Kafelnikov— as this historic and momentous Davis Cup year reached its climax.

SEMIFINAL ROUND

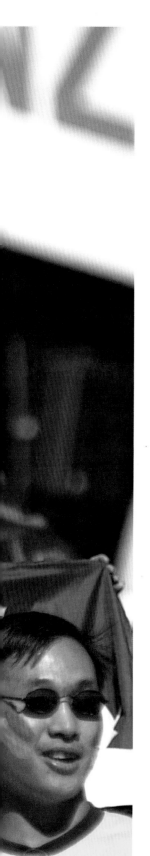

A DATE WITH DESTINY

Semifinals are, by their nature, fraught occasions, usually so close they pluck at the nerves and wrench the guts. So near to the Final but in the same way so very far, they are often decided in the last minute, either by a moment of genius or an error that lives with the perpetrator for eons.

But not this year. The 2000 Davis Cup featured two 5–0 whitewashes, utterly comprehensive in their manner, disdainful and hurtful in equal measure. There was brutality in Brisbane and slaughter in Santander.

From the moment John McEnroe managed to unravel the complexities of the draw—and it takes some unraveling even for a man of his intelligence—he suspected America's fate would come down to a semifinal summer showdown with Spain in Spain on clay. The prospect chilled him. Zimbabwe, for all its perils, would be nothing compared to the welcome awaiting McEnroe and his less-than-merry men when they landed on the northern coastline of the Iberian Peninsula.

Once again, the United States' prospects were blighted from the moment McEnroe started to assemble a team. Andre Agassi had decreed in a conversation with a knot of British writers just before Wimbledon that Spain away represented "a nightmare" for him. Even after he reached the semifinal at the All England Club, there were those who questioned the depth of his resolve to compete on clay two weeks later.

On his way home from the Las Vegas airport, Agassi was involved in an alleged shunt with another vehicle and was ruled out of participation on the advice of the U.S. team doctor George Fareed, who cited a "hyperextension injury of the mid- and lower-back and muscular spasms on the right side of his spine that prohibit him from raising his right arm above his shoulder." McEnroe could not argue with that one; nor could he insist that Pete Sampras make the trip back to Europe. It was too soon after his seventh victory at Wimbledon, a win that took him to the precipice of physical and mental exhaustion.

The U.S. struggles without its strongest team.

above Captain John McEnroe was unable to inspire Todd Martin and an understrength U.S. team to victory over Spain.

previous spread Even away from home, the Australian supporters make themselves heard in Brisbane.

So what was to become of the American team? Todd Martin had represented his country every year since 1994 but missed the first round tie in Zimbabwe with a viral infection and the second round tie against the Czech Republic with a severely sprained ankle. He should have taken Agassi out in an incredible second round meeting at Wimbledon, when he served for the match twice from a 5–2 lead in the fifth set. Although Martin is an exceptional player, his performance in critical situations is somewhat questionable and Santander would be difficult.

Jan-Michael Gambill had reached Wimbledon's last eight and shown that he was not fazed by big-time occasions in two appearances on Centre Court—in the opening round against Lleyton Hewitt and the quarters against Sampras. Did he have the mettle for a Davis Cup tie that would test his resolve to the limits? McEnroe hoped so.

There were rumors that the captain himself might play, so when McEnroe tagged himself as the fourth player in the initial choice on July 11, the Spanish hosts expected to be inundated with late requests for media applications. McEnroe back in a semifinal of the Davis Cup at age forty-one was a prospect that had sports editors across the world drooling.

"I've actually been trying to reach a couple of other players but I haven't been able to, so this is a stop-gap solution," McEnroe explained. "I'd say there's a good chance I won't play but there's also a chance I will. If we can pull this one out of the hat, it will be a real victory."

Eventually, Vince Spadea returned McEnroe's call, and the idea that the captain might step out onto the court receded. But he still had the problem of deciding whether Martin—who had been stricken with injury—could possibly play two singles and a doubles in what were certain to be debilitating conditions.

You could tell that the mood in the U.S. camp was touchy at the opening draw ceremony, held on the grounds of the spectacular Magdalena Royal Palace, a castle that looked to have been transplanted from Disney World. The U.S. team was dressed to kill in temperatures touching 90 degrees; they sweated and, inwardly, they cursed. The captain's dissatisfaction with the quality at his disposal was clear for all to see. But he hoped that his body language didn't seep through to his players.

As it was, few gave the Americans much of a chance. Things were going too well for the Spanish. Two of their team, Alex Corretja and Albert Costa, had boycotted Wimbledon in an argument over their seedings and while everyone else was exerting themselves on grass, they spent the time getting their feet dirtier on the clay.

Corretja, arguably his country's most famous contemporary player, won the championship in Gstaad the week before Davis Cup so there was no denying his readiness. Costa had reached the quarterfinal of Roland Garros in 2000, and Spain also had at its disposal Juan Carlos Ferrero, the twenty-year-old who had underscored his extraordinary talents by getting to the semifinals of the French Open on his first appearance in the main draw.

What could McEnroe expect, even in his most wildly optimistic dreams? An upset, a miracle was what he hoped for.

It was a pity his players could not indulge a little in the peaceful charm of the surroundings. From the rather grimy port end of town, Santander rises to its western fringe in a flurry of delightful seafood restaurants

and spotlessly clean, expansive beaches. These would have been perfect places for the Americans to chill out, ease into the atmosphere, and enjoy the richness of the European culture. They might even have had some fun.

The Spanish were thrilled to have the Americans on their patch. Twelve thousand five hundred tickets had sold out within five hours of going on sale. Local people erected a purpose-built facility in what passed for the back garden of the Real Sociedad de Tennis de la Magdalena, a wonderful club that sat on an isthmus between the Bay of Biscay and the waters surrounding the golfing idyll of Penina, spiritual home of the legendary Severiano Ballesteros.

It was 1967 when Spain had last reached a Davis Cup Final—about as remarkable a statistic as was the fact that Italy had never been relegated from the World Group. They knew this was their finest opportunity—there was a bonding in their team that McEnroe could only dream of, a sense of togetherness that went unanswered when they looked into the eyes of the opposition.

The Americans tried their best to be upbeat. McEnroe was still talking about dusting down his racket but had ultimately been talked out of competing by those who believed he would embarrass himself. "We beat him up a little bit," said Gambill. "We told him we might desert him if he played." Woodruff chipped in that he had been having a field day with McEnroe's second serve in practice. The prospect of seeing the old man in his whites was put in perspective by Martin, who said: "John is not head and shoulders above us in the caliber of doubles players right now, but his knowledge of the game is better. I think he will be at his best on the sidelines."

Faced with such common sense, McEnroe stepped back. "I'll have to wait till the Final," he said, but the humor was not as bright as it might have been. The American party hardly overflowed with optimism, though they spoke a decent-enough game. Woodruff recited his Zimbabwean experience as a reason to be cheerful. Gambill said that with his Wimbledon breakthrough, he had "figured out how to win." Spadea insisted that although his ranking had fallen through the floor, "I'm still one of the top players in America." Martin was as "eager as I've ever been. We're raring to get going." Martin knew that his performance in the opening singles against Costa would set the trend of the tie. He had more experience than the rest of the side put together, and he had won a tournament on Spanish clay. In fact, his record against Spanish players was positively awe-inspiring.

Martin knew that his best form of attack was . . . attack. It was a game plan that required cunning and courage, but the temperatures on the court made up Martin's mind for him. After all, he was a player who had suffered terribly before in similar conditions and he knew he couldn't afford to let Costa into the match.

Martin won the first seven points—the magic eighth eluded him. Costa sprung the trap and never looked back. Had the veteran in the peaked cap broken once in the first set or been able to cement a 2–0 lead at the start of the second, he might have made Costa stretch a little more. But as the Spaniard took his next three service games, Martin was visibly wilting under the strain of it all and he simply did not have the inspiration required. A 6–4, 6–4, 6–4 defeat was wildly celebrated by the Spanish team.

"I had 0–40 twice in the first set and he got out of those games," Martin reflected. "Not only that, he got out of them quickly and that was a big lift for him and tough for me to have to deal with. I'm a big believer that the way you start a match sends a message. From one game and 0–40, I overcooked a forehand and then he starts to play loose.

"I felt Albert returned my serves as well as he ever has. I began to get caught off balance with a few of his bad returns, too, which put me into some strange positions."

The position for McEnroe was anything but strange—he simply had to hope that Gambill could cope with a desperate situation in his first Davis Cup tie on foreign soil. The young kid's reaction was admirable. He shot through the first set in thirty-one minutes, breaking Corretja twice, and had two break points for a 2–1 lead in the second. The crowd seized the moment, chanting "Alex! Alex!" in a desperate attempt to rouse their lion-hearted champion.

Corretja, in response, turned the screw a notch. Gambill's play didn't fall far beneath the level of the opening set—Corretja's simply became so much steadier. The points became ever longer and longer, wringing every ounce of stamina from Gambill's superbly honed frame. He kept telling himself to stay patient and wait for his chance, but the sweat was trickling into his eyes and soaking his clothes.

As the match wore on, McEnroe became increasingly subdued and it was Duarte—normally so collected when he watches Corretja play on the regular tour—who was leaping out of his chair in moments of exuberance and exhibitionism.

Slowly but surely, Corretja's grip grew more secure and his 1–6, 6–3, 6–4, 6–4 victory gave Spain a comfortable first-night lead.

left Jan-Michael Gambill made a flying start against Alex Corretja before going down in four sets.

above Albert Costa enjoyed a straight sets triumph over Todd Martin.

Gambill came in to face the media—four Americans, two Brits, and a sackful of Spaniards—and would not be sidetracked by well-meaning gestures. "I'm pissed at the world," he said. "I didn't want to come here and lose—I don't care who I'm playing. I played hard and gave it 100 percent, and just didn't come up with a win. It's bigger than a loss because I had my whole country behind me.

"I think that I'll do well in the future of the Davis Cup. I know I'll be on the team for many years to come and I'm going to learn from this. These guys are tough, this is their surface—on anything else we'd have an advantage. The crowd was irrelevant to me—they weren't hostile, they didn't affect me."

McEnroe had to patch up and move on. Two down and a doubles team likely to consist of Martin, who was playing from memory. "The one thing I'm not going to do is say, 'That's it, I quit,' if we lose," McEnroe said. "I might have made spur-of-the-moment statements like that when I was younger.

"I'm letting the situation sink in, giving me time to dwell on the positive. It's just like my own career. When I realize this is a great job I'll think about the positives but it's hard tonight." And it would get harder the following day.

That evening, the United States Tennis Association hosted a dinner party attended by their president Judy Levering, who had summoned the courage to appoint McEnroe in the first place. "I have slipped a note under his door tonight, because I know he'll be down and I want to make sure he knows we are fully support-ive of him," she said. "It has been a disappointing day, but all is not lost."

Alex Corretja could have been in church the way he sang throughout the warm-up on Stadium Court with Juan Balcells, the tennis player with the most intimidating set of sideburns in the world. Would the Spaniards

require any divine intervention? On a court tucked behind the clubhouse, John McEnroe half-watched Martin and Chris Woodruff but was distracted by the rigorous workout of Juan Carlos Ferrero, the little god of Spanish tennis.

McEnroe couldn't believe that the U.S. was about to be knocked out by the Spanish team without Ferrero, arguably its finest young player, and Carlos Moya, the only Spaniard in the top 40 who had won a Grand Slam title. He gulped a little and tried to think if there was any way he could persuade Martin and Woodruff to play the doubles match of their lives.

For a while it seemed they were doing just that. The Corretja serve that had faltered in the first set of his singles against Gambill succumbed twice in the opening set, and though Woodruff had given one break back, Martin served for it at 5–4. The next few minutes were to become a microcosm of America's blighted weekend. On break point, Woodruff responded with a decisive volley. A set point for the U.S. was saved by a blistering Corretja backhand service return. On Spain's second break point, Woodruff failed to control a backhand volley that sailed into the dust beyond the baseline, leveling the set at 5–all.

A second set point on Balcells's serve was denied the Americans when Martin netted a backhand return. The Americans saved two break points on the Woodruff serve and forced a tiebreak. In the breaker it went with serve until Balcells's double-fault at 4–5 gave the American team two more set points. Corretja saved the first with a fulminating smash; Balcells the second with a brave interception. After another instinctive move at the net by Balcells, Spain took the tiebreak 8–6.

The Americans gritted their teeth and fought back, taking the second set 6–2. The start of the third set was the time for Corretja to play like the senior partner and so he did, excelling in the conditions, whipping both the crowd and his cohort to new heights. Spain won the third set but Martin and Woodruff would not lie down, taking the fourth on a tiebreak.

The start of the fifth was explosive as the Spaniards raced to a 3–0 lead. But the U.S. pulled it back to 3–3, though the effort required to keep the game alive began to have its effect. The Woodruff serve was plundered in the eighth game, leaving Corretja to serve for one of the most magical moments of his life.

Spain was in the Final for the first time in more than three decades. Why? "Because we flow along the same lines," said Corretja at the press conference. "We want to keep the compact group we have right now. The four of us here, we are very proud with all the captains and the members of the team. Perhaps the four of us here will not be in the Final, we don't know, but we've started history and we want to go on with history.

"I believe this is the first time that we're not going to step in the locker room and the guys say, 'Aaahh, Spanish guys, you are good players on the Tour, but you don't know how to win the Davis Cup.' We are in the Final now. We fought for it and we are here."

The Americans trooped in, all looking a little grayer than when they had started. McEnroe tried to stir up a little plot by suggesting the Spaniards had watered the court when the Americans knew nothing about it, but he wasn't really convincing about it. If his heart had been in the argument, he would have been proper raging. "We have to overcome these things ultimately," he said. "They watered the court, but we should have won anyway. We left the court for five minutes at the end of the fourth set and maybe we lost a little focus.

Hopefully things will get easier next year. This has been a tough indoctrination."

The last question McEnroe was asked referred to Sampras and Agassi. Had he received any message from them? "Nope," he replied sullenly. "I'm amazed it took you guys so long to get around to those two," said Martin, the air heavy with sarcasm. Neither Sampras or Agassi could make it, but their impact—or lack of it—was surely felt.

AUSTRALIA AT HOME ON GRASS

Halfway around the world, another captain's mood was far from mellow. The first-round defeat of Lleyton Hewitt by Jan-Michael Gambill at Wimbledon aside, there was plenty for John Newcombe to be content with. Patrick Rafter had reached his first final on the Wimbledon lawns, only to stumble when leading by a set and 4–1 in the second set tiebreak with two serves to come.

Mark Philippoussis, having survived an extraordinary five-hour match with Sjeng Schalken of Holland on the middle Saturday of the Championships, had defeated the Englishman Tim Henman, but found Sampras too clever in the quarters. For Australia, there was enough grass court practice in there—Hewitt had won at Queen's Club, beating Sampras, and reached the final of the mixed at Wimbledon—for Newcombe not to fret over the threat posed by Brazil in Brisbane.

But trouble of another kind was looming. There was Philippoussis with his track record of tournament truancy. Australia had long been versed in his tendency to undermine team planning by pulling out when mood or injury took him. He had done much to repair his image by starring in the 1999 Final and then

holding the team together in the opening round of the 2000 competition in Zurich. But few held out the hope that such consistency would last long.

Thus, when Philippoussis chose the day after Wimbledon—when Australia was chorusing its disappointment over Rafter's loss to Sampras—to announce he wasn't fit for the semifinal, the anger was palpable.

Tennis Australia duly issued a statement saying that Philippoussis had withdrawn, citing an inflammation in his right knee. The same day, Colin Stubs, tournament director of the Colonial Classic, a pre-Australian Open exhibition, chose to announce that he would not invite Philippoussis to play in this popular event again. Philippoussis had reached the Colonial final in 2000 and then pulled out with a neck strain, leaving Stubs stranded. For that, Stubs condemned him as "unprofessional."

The returning Rafter, exhausted by his Wimbledon exploits, heard the news about Philippoussis and Brisbane after twenty-four hours in the air. "I guess he doesn't feel like playing Davis Cup; I wish he'd come out and say something, just to clear the air. I'd respect him a lot more if he did that instead of jerking us around."

The inference was clear. Rafter was laying himself on the line, Philippoussis was lying on his back. "Davis Cup brings out a lot of emotion and you get a lot of energy from it," said the Australian favorite. "It's team sport and I love playing team sport. It's always a lot of fun being with the boys and playing for your country. I'd like to sort out my differences with Mark—I'd just like to see how he views it."

Philippoussis stood his ground, insisting that everything had been blown out of proportion and he would never deliberately withdraw from the Davis Cup unless he was injured. The Aussies decided to put the controversy behind them and get on with the task at hand—defeating Brazil.

Captain Newcombe discussed their challenge. "Lleyton hasn't played singles since the first day of Wimbledon, so his nervous system hasn't been at a high pitch, whereas Pat's was running high until 9 p.m. last Sunday evening in London when he finished a Wimbledon final, got on a plane the next day, and traveled down to Australia. After you've been at that level for so long, your nervous system says, 'Give me a break.' At least Pat doesn't have to acclimatize to a surface change."

Newcombe knew that Rafter would be ready. What he couldn't bargain for was how Gustavo Kuerten— brilliant on clay, getting better all the time on hard court, but an unknown entity on grass—could react at the ANZ Stadium. "He's going to come in guts, feathers, and all," said Newcombe. "He's won the French Open, has a great Davis Cup singles record, and he's won 10 out of 11 doubles. If you go onto court thinking he's not a threat, you're stupid."

Rafter would meet Kuerten at 9:30 on Friday morning. "Are you a morning person?" the Brazilian was asked. After a long pause, he said dryly: "I'm afraid not. But we have to find a way to get to the Davis Cup Final."

Rafter picked up in Brisbane where he had left off in London. Jetlag notwithstanding, Rafter won 6–3, 6–2, 6–3 in eighty-one minutes, never allowing Kuerten, troubled by a groin injury, to settle and slicing through his defenses. Hewitt picked up the baton and defeated Fernando Meligeni 6–4, 6–2, 6–3, showing that he was not only more solid from the back of the court but that his net game had improved under the common-sense control of his coach, Darren Cahill.

Besides Hewitt's dominance, Meligeni was not helped by some erratic line calls. Whatever way he looked at it—and at one point he stood on his head—he was getting a thrashing.

In his six ties for Australia, Hewitt had a record of 8–3 in singles. "I did what I had to do without playing brilliantly," was Hewitt's assertion. "When I needed to feel pumped, I did a little fist to myself—there was no overreaction. I knew I needed to keep my emotions in check."

Newcombe knew that Brazil was on the ropes. Now was the moment to finish them off. The captain resisted the temptation to play Rafter in the doubles with Mark Woodforde and stuck with his original selection of the ginger-one and Sandon Stolle. Brazil needed a risk strategy and their Captain Ricardo Acioly knew Kuerten had to play to give his side a chance of pulling the semi around.

In partnership with the Dutchman Paul Haarhuis, Stolle had figured in two Grand Slam finals in 2000 at Roland Garros and Wimbledon, losing both to the Woodies. Now he had the chance to partner Woodforde, knowing that if the team lost, there would be those who would wonder whether Todd Woodbridge shouldn't have been nominated for such an important tie.

Kuerten, in collaboration with Jaime Oncins, began in his trademark loose-as-a-goose style, pounding down an ace to help his country win the first set on a tiebreak. His serve, though, was captured in the third game of the second set, allowing the Aussies to draw level, but Woodforde faltered in the third set, giving Brazil a two-sets-to-one lead.

Each time one of the four stepped forward, the pressure was ratcheted up a few notches. In the seventh game of the fourth set, Oncins was serving 0–40. The Brazilians hauled the points back, but Oncins double-faulted on a fifth break point and, once more, the rubber was tied. Stolle found himself serving for the match, and he stood resolute.

Where as in Nice seven months earlier, it had been the dark-haired Philippoussis who was borne around the court on his teammates' shoulders, this time it was the dark-haired Sandon Stolle who had finally broken out of the shadow of his father Fred, a member of three championship winning sides of the sixties. "All of us wanted it for Sandon," said Captain Newcombe, "because he's had some real bitter defeats. This is the turning point, mate, you're a winner now." And so said all of Australia.

Hewitt and Rafter completed the whitewash in the reverse singles in straight sets over Andre Sa and Meligeni. The Brazilians had been well and truly thrashed and the Aussies were typically undaunted by the prospect of successfully defending the trophy for the first time in thirty-three years on clay in Spain. They had done it in Nice, why not Barcelona?

Whether Philippoussis would be there or not hardly mattered this weekend, but Hewitt could not help offering some advice. "A lot of things have to be sorted out," he said. "With a new captain and coach coming in next year [John Fitzgerald and Wally Masur], it's going to be a whole different ball game. They are going to have to set the law down right from the start. You have to put yourself on the line every time for your country. You can't be in and out.

"Maybe we can fix [the problem with Philippoussis] for the future. We want to know if we've done something wrong as a team. He would be great to have in our team in the future, for sure, but he has to mend a lot of things before he comes back on."

Not for the last time, the ball was firmly in the court of Mark Philippoussis.

above Sandon Stolle was Australia's hero as he broke his Davis Cup doubles duck by partnering Mark Woodforde to a five-set victory over Gustavo Kuerten and Jaime Oncins.

PATRICK RAFTER

profile *Patrick Rafter* | **birthplace** *Mount Isa, Queensland* | **birthdate** 12•28•72 | **turned professional** 1991 | **Davis Cup records** *singles* 14–8 • *doubles* 2–0

"I SUPPOSE I'M ONE OF THE OLDER GUYS NOW AND I NEVER THOUGHT I'D HEAR MYSELF SAY THAT."

"Pat Rafter is the most unchanged guy I know who made it big in sport," said John Fitzgerald, the captain-elect of the Australian Davis Cup team. It was praise indeed coming from someone who found fame on the tennis court and remained a mate in every sense of the word. And it is, without doubt, a true and genuine reflection of a player who has accepted the slings and arrows of outrageous injury misfortune in the past couple of years and treated his triumphs and disasters just the same.

There is at least one—quite possibly more—female tennis correspondent on the circuit whose computer screen is filled with images of the Aussie hunk. "The loveliest butt in the world," she swoons. Rafter would probably blanche at the thought, but equally, he knows his attraction to the ladies makes him one of the most marketable people in the sport.

The great thing about Pat Rafter is that fame has never gone to his head—and never will. He is exactly the kind of personable person that men's tennis has needed these past few years—a highly talented athlete who appreciates what the game has meant to him and who gives back all of it and more. There is no more proud Aussie—no one in the game to whom the Davis Cup means as much.

"I appreciate the richness of the tradition in Australia that has been handed down from the likes of Neale Fraser, Rod Laver, Roy Emerson, John Newcombe, and Tony Roche—all the great Aussies," he says. "They have set us such a high standard. They are such wonderful people to have as role models."

Rafter continues the legacy. Having been the third youngest of nine children has helped him keep a sense of perspective. "He is still the same kid who beat about with his five brothers back home in Queensland," said Fitzgerald. "He grew up in the kind of family environment that taught love and discipline at the same time. He was never allowed to get away with anything and has kept to that example."

With almost $10 million in the bank in prize money alone, Rafter has become a supporter and fundraiser extraordinaire. After he won the US Open title in 1997, he donated $300,000 to the Brisbane Mater Hospital. Having repeated his victory at Flushing Meadows a year later, he repeated the donation, this time to the Starlight Foundation Express Room for terminally ill children. The Patrick Rafter Cherish the Children Foundation, officially launched last year and run by his sister Louise, was named as one of the three charities of the Olympic Games, something of which he was immensely proud.

In Australia, there is no more popular sportsman and at twenty-eight, he appreciates the time he has had at the highest reaches of the sport he loves. He spends a lot of it these days listening to his body creak and groan. "It's a day-to-day thing. There are good days and bad, and on the bad ones, you don't go out and push it," he said, referring to the shoulder injury that required arthroscopic surgery in October 1999.

"When I had my time off I wasn't missing the game very much. I always wondered what I would do if I didn't play tennis anymore, and nothing came to mind, so I was in limbo. I always thought I'd be able to get back into it and play again. I still like to have my fun and there are times maybe when I do things I shouldn't, but when it comes to doing the work, I'm not afraid to do it."

It is no surprise that the press loves him, though he has had his moments. "The little skirmishes blow over, though," he says. "I always remember Newk saying if someone writes a bad article just pat them on the back and say next time write a better article, there's no point going up to someone saying 'You b*****,' otherwise they'll keep writing bad articles. I've tried to have that attitude with the press."

Rafter's schedule has always included Davis Cup and will until the day he hangs up his Prince. He says he likes the idea of the ATP's Tennis Masters Series that began in 2000, but would not be playing them all. There has to be room for the priority events, and he has to keep fit to see off the teenage threat. "The kids are going to get up for it but I'm still happy with my ability. I suppose I'm one of the older guys now and I never thought I'd hear myself say that."

WORLD GROUP QUALIFYING ROUND

Ecuador d. Great Britain • *London, England* | Belgium d. Italy • *Mestre, Italy* | France d. Austria • *Rennes, France*

Switzerland d. Belarus • *St. Gallen, Switzerland* | Romania d. Zimbabwe • *Harare, Zimbabwe* | Sweden d. India •

Bastad, Sweden | Netherlands d. Uzbekistan • *Tashkent, Uzbekistan* | *matches played July 14–16 and July 21–23,* 2000

BROTHERS IN ARMS

Roger Taylor looked out across the verdant fields of the Bank of England sports ground at the ITF offices in Roehampton on the April morning of the World Group Qualifying Round draw. Everything in his world seemed just as lush and fertile.

Of all the ties Taylor might have been granted for his baptism as David Lloyd's replacement as Britain's captain, out came a comparative plum—Ecuador at home. The prospects had been bleak, for the Davis Cup replica cup from which the potential nations would be drawn was overflowing with banana-skinned possibilities: trips to Europe's outer reaches, South America, or the Asian subcontinent to negotiate the week following Wimbledon. Instead, Taylor could look forward to a very winnable tie, and the London grass never seemed greener.

The International Tennis Federation had relocated from its offices in Baron's Court to the prime spot in West London where the English soccer team prepared for the 1966 World Cup. Bobby Charlton, Bobby Moore, and company had warmed up on the grassy knolls of Roehampton before setting out to conquer the world.

Now was the time to pinch oneself and imagine British tennis taking the same quantum leap.

The venue for the Ecuador tie was decided within twenty-four hours. The Number One court at the All England Club, built in 1996, was to have its first taste of the competition's magic, in the hope that British supporters would generate a level of noise reminiscent of the championship's famous "people's days," when ordinary folk took precedence over the corporate chosen.

It could have been a whole lot worse, was the gist of Taylor's reaction. He made the right diplomatic noises, but there was no doubting his inner sense of well-being. He knew about Nicolas Lapentti, the glamour boy of tennis in Ecuador, who ended 1999 ranked 8th in the world. Lapentti's leap of eighty-four spots on the ATP Tour was the second best since rankings were established in 1973. He was a semifinalist at the 2000 Australian Open, but his results on grass were not impressive.

from left to right One of the younger British fans gets behind her team. British Captain Roger Taylor saw Arvind Parmar squander a two-set lead in the deciding rubber.

previous spread Wimbledon's Number 1 Court saw a record attendance for a Davis Cup tie in Great Britain.

There were also rumors that Nicolas's younger brother Giovanni was a teenage phenomenon, but none of the British writers had seen him play, so it was little more than the language of the grapevine. Of the rest of the squad, most confessed to knowing nothing at all.

This was Taylor's first taste of Davis Cup in the role he wished he had been given years earlier. He made his final appearance in the competition as a player a quarter of a century earlier, having played eighteen ties over seven years, winning twenty-six singles, and losing nine—an impressive record of quality and endurance.

The candidates for the job were thin on the ground. Patrice Hagelauer, the Lawn Tennis Association's performance director who had coached the French team to their Davis Cup victories in 1991 and 1996, was not an option because he didn't hold a British passport and hadn't lived in Britain for two years (two requirements for the Davis Cup captain). None of the players who had retired in the recent past—Jeremy Bates, Mark Petchey, or Chris Bailey—possessed requisite experience.

Eventually, the LTA plumped for Taylor, whose reputation as a performance coach working with some of Britain's best youngsters had been steadily growing. It obviously helped that he frequently played golf near his tennis ranch in Portugal with Tim Henman's parents, Jane and Tony. Paul Hutchins, a former Davis Cup captain, thought him an excellent choice.

"Roger was a great fighter," Hutchins said. "I can remember him being within a point of beating Manuel Orantes on clay in Barcelona in the final rubber, with the scores tied at 2–2. He played a brilliant chipped backhand we all thought was a winner but Orantes reached it and played a wonderful shot down the line with his eyes closed. It was a phenomenal effort."

Hutchins offered Taylor a piece of advice. "It is obviously crucial for him to get to know the players and their respective coaches as quickly as possible. The television cameras are on you during changeovers in the Davis Cup and if as the captain you sit there and don't say anything, you look a proper Charlie."

That had never been Lloyd's way, and when it came time for the LTA to sack him, he reacted as he had throughout his life. He refused to go quietly.

"I'm proud of what I've done with the team," he said. "We won eight of eleven matches and only lost once when I had both Tim Henman and Greg Rusedski to choose from, which isn't a bad record.

"We've had to build a team around two strong personalities who have not always got along and I actually had them communicating and playing doubles together. I've been sacrificed for I don't know what, but it was only a matter of time from when I was appointed. There are lots of people at the LTA who have failed time and time again and they're scared of me. I would have gone after the next tie anyway because the job had completely changed.

"Basically, the Davis Cup captain sits on court, pours the drinks, and peels the bananas. He's only a figurehead, while the coach's job is completely redundant."

Taylor and Lloyd may have been related by marriage—Taylor's former wife Frances was Lloyd's sister-in-law—but they were far removed as personalities. Taylor, too, was no stranger to spats with the LTA over fitness (the issue Lloyd had raised in Australia after the defeats of Jamie Delgado and Arvind Parmar). After coaching the Wightman Cup women's team to their famous victory over the United States at the Royal Albert Hall in 1978, Taylor was asked to step down when the players complained he worked them too hard. And Taylor was no pillar of the establishment, having clawed his way up from the public parks to forge a career as a powerful left-hander with an abrasive style.

He would need some of that abrasion in the weeks to come, as the British camp was not a happy one. Rusedski, for instance, had spent over a month leading the British media a merry dance about his availability for the Ecuador tie. Lloyd had been a guest at Rusedski's wedding the previous Christmas and so perhaps one could understand the outraged reaction to his departure. But it was Henman who had been discovered by a private tennis initiative in the mid-eighties that had been promoted and partially financed by Lloyd, so it would have seemed that he, not Rusedski, would champion Lloyd.

Besides his off-court unhappiness, Rusedski also struggled on court, losing in the first round at Roland Garros and insisting he would never darken the doors of red clay again. Then he was defeated by Vince Spadea in a five-set slugfest on Number One court at Wimbledon in the opening round—the same Spadea who entered the Championships having not won a singles since October. Rusedski's whole mood was one of melancholy with the Ecuador tie three weeks away, which boded poorly for Taylor's campaign.

Henman's progress was halted in the last sixteen by a bludgeoning performance from Australia's Mark Philippoussis at Wimbledon, but he was far happier. The elder Lapentti lost in the first round of Wimbledon, his brother was beaten in the second round of the boys' singles, and of Luis Morejon the sages knew absolutely nothing, but the Ecuadorians used their time off to learn to play on grass. The Davis Cup draw pitted Rusedski first against Nicolas Lapentti, with Henman to follow against Morejon; Henman and Rusedski were named as the doubles team; and the Lapentti brothers would appear for Ecuador.

Even at home, no one gave the South Americans much of a chance. In listing twenty things its readers ought to know about Ecuador before the tie, the *London Times* mentioned that it had eight active volcanoes (more than there were British men in the top 200), that it once had four presidents in sixteen days, and that Panama hats are actually made in the Ecuadorian city of Monte Cristo.

It seemed like sour grapes when the sacked Lloyd declared—obviously in a fit of unashamed pique—that a blind school could defeat Ecuador on grass. Taking the higher road, Taylor said his team was "very disappointed" at the remarks. "We have to keep the spirit and goodwill of the Davis Cup alive and things like this don't help," he added. The British press fed on the comments for all they were worth.

Day one dawned blustery and cool for mid-July and it was impossible to tell whether or not Rusedski was happy to be back on Court One. Demons were all around. Nicolas Lapentti, who had been quoted as saying some uncharitable things about his opponent, didn't appear the slightest bit intimidated. He took the first set, then led by two sets to one, and though he was 2–0 down in the fifth, he never panicked.

The more he started to nail the Rusedski serve, the more anxious the British import and the crowd became—a fear that pervaded the court and seeped into your bones, like the bitter cold of the wind. Serving at 5–6 in the fifth, Rusedski's seventh double-fault gave Lapentti two match points and a booming backhand service return, completely lacking inhibition, secured a famous victory.

Lapentti's first reaction was to distance himself from his pre-match comments. "I don't know who wrote that I had bad things to say about Greg because he is a great guy," he insisted. "If he is not having a good moment right now I don't want him to think I have said anything bad ... so I apologize." (Though, for what, he didn't elaborate.)

"There was huge history and tradition about me playing on this court for Ecuador. It is tough to describe what feelings I had playing there. When I played in South Africa, I felt they got personal with the players but there was none of that here."

But, as we would see later, things were getting a little too personal for Rusedski. His defeat might have heaped pressure on Henman, but the number 1 didn't show it, sweeping past Morejon—who looked completely shell-shocked—in straight sets. The tie was all square at 1–1 with Henman and Rusedski due to meet the Lapenttis on Saturday afternoon. But rumors that Rusedski would withdraw were confirmed an hour before the match when the British camp announced their team would be Henman and Parmar. What was the matter with Rusedski? He came into a press conference to announce that the foot injury that had hindered him for almost a year was troubling him again and that he would be heading back to Germany for another session with the eminent surgeon Hans Muller Wolfahrt.

Henman rarely plays doubles other than in Davis Cup, so he and Parmar were not well equipped for such a vital match. The Lapenttis had siblings' sixth sense—after all, they were raised together. Doubles tennis was as natural to them as riding tandem.

The result was a shocker for the home team. The Lapenttis won in straight sets, while the Brits played like relative strangers. Taylor, who had looked forward with such hope to his debut, now knew his re-jigged team had to win the remaining two singles to stay in the World Group.

Henman kept his end of the bargain by playing near-faultless singles in his dashing grass-court style to

defeat the elder Lapentti in straight sets. And after the opening two sets of the final singles, both pocketed by Parmar against Giovanni Lapentti, the signs were that the home crowd had been worrying needlessly. Even if he was far from completely convincing, Parmar surely had enough to win the one more set that was crucial to the short-term stability of tennis in Britain.

Ecuador's captain, Raul Viver, had chosen the younger Lapentti ahead of Morejon for the final rubber, and it was beginning to look as though his brave decision had backfired. Exactly how the transformation came about, no one could be sure. The nerveless teenager had struck the ball well all afternoon but now his passing shots were beginning to have real penetration. Parmar had not looked comfortable at the net and as games slipped by, his nerves gripped him. His long limbs tightened, and he began to take shorter and shorter breaths. He was choking.

Parmar lost in five sets to the crowd's dismay. The entire Ecuadorian troupe clambered over the low walls of Number One court to crush its seventeen-year-old hero in the middle of one of the most sacred pieces of grass in the kingdom. Lapentti was in floods of tears in his press conference, and Parmar was shell-shocked. Within hours, Richard Lewis, a former Davis Cupper, resigned as Britain's director of tennis. The fallout would reverberate for months, maybe years to come.

ITALIAN RUN ENDED

The shadows lengthening over British tennis were casting their gloom further afield across the continent of Europe. Italy, the 1998 finalists, shared with the Czech Republic the distinction of never having been relegated from the World Group—an extraordinary achievement, given that they had not possessed a player of huge influence for three decades.

from left to right Christophe Rochus and Tom Van Houdt celebrate Belgium's doubles victory over Italy. Davide Sanguinetti is inconsolable after his five-set defeat by Christophe Rochus saw Italy relegated from the World Group for the first time.

Rino Tommasi, one of the three masters of Italian tennis literature (the engaging triumvirate of Tommasi, Gianni Clerici, and Ubaldo Scanagatta have probably attended more Davis Cup ties than the rest of the world's media put together), was one of those who wondered how Italy had kept its head above water for so long. "We have been a weak nation for many years but we have survived by one means or another," he said.

"We told the Italian people to be prepared for this to happen but only when it did happen did they realize what we had all been saying for a long time. There is a crisis in Italian tennis and maybe this will help us to address it properly."

If reaching the 1998 Davis Cup Final was considered something of a fluke (the United States' performance in the semifinals in Milwaukee was nothing short of miserable, allowing Italy to get through), then losing to Belgium in the 2000 World Group Qualifying Round in Mestre was the rudest of awakenings. And they didn't lose to a nation, but a family. This was the coming of age of Belgium's Rochus boys, Christophe and Olivier.

Nothing much had gone right for Andrea Gaudenzi since the Final in Milan where he battled heroically against a shoulder injury that caused him to pull up at 6–6 in the fifth set of an extraordinary tussle against Magnus Norman of Sweden. He finished 1999 as the Italian number 1 for the fifth time in six years, despite missing the first three months of the season to the debilitating implications of the problem with his serving shoulder.

From his career high ranking of 22 at the end of 1995, he had struggled to stay within the top 50 and was now perilously close to dropping out of the leading 100 players. Indeed, by the time the tie against

Belgium came around, Gaudenzi was ranked exactly 100th in the ATP Tour's entry system, which evaluates performance over fifty-two weeks.

Gaudenzi was drawn to face the nineteen-year-old Olivier Rochus, the younger of the brothers, who both made up for their lack of physical stature with the size of their hearts. Rochus, a former semifinalist at Junior Wimbledon, had reached the third round of the 2000 Championships proper. He defeated French Open finalist Norman before losing to another Italian, Gianluca Pozzi, and then went on to win a Challenger event the week preceding Davis Cup. Here was a teenager on fire and so Belgian captain Gabriel Gonzalez asked him to play a live singles for the first time in his life.

Rochus responded to the challenge with maturity beyond his years. "I felt very confident going into the match," he said. "I knew it was going to be tough against Andrea because he had the crowd on his side and nobody really gave Belgium a chance. I was cramping in the third set but I think that was more to do with nerves than anything else. It was very close but I held on." He held on to win 6–2, 7–5, 6–3, in fact, and provide the first of what would be a number of seismic shocks through the host country.

Davide Sanguinetti was also trying to haul his ranking back to acceptable levels after finishing 1999 outside the top 100 for the first time in three years. It was proving to be no easy ride, especially with the substantial expectation Italy placed on him. He had recovered back into the eighties, largely due to a compelling week on grass at London's Queen's Club where he reached the semifinals, only to lose to Pete Sampras in two close sets.

But the two atmospheres could hardly be aligned—the clinking glasses of Queen's and the clanking of Belgian hooves. Sanguinetti was a set down to Filip Dewulf before he knew what had hit him, but he recovered to take the second set tiebreak, hold his nerve in the third set, and speed away to bring the tie level at 1–1. Even so, deep in Italian hearts, there was a feeling that his 1–6, 7–6, 7–5, 6–0 victory was merely a delay of the inevitable.

Christophe Rochus and Tom Van Houdt combined to defeat Gaudenzi and the veteran Diego Nargiso in straight sets in the doubles to provide the Belgians with a lead for the second time. Gonzalez then made a critical move, for though Christophe had played on the Saturday, the captain felt he and not his younger sibling would handle the pressure a little better. It was a hunch out of the Viver class.

Rochus led Sanguinetti two sets to love but the Italian with the gray-flecked movie star looks would not fold and won a breathtaking third set tiebreak 8–6. "I was really down mentally after that third set," recalled Rochus, who was reeling when Sanguinetti pocketed the fourth 6–1 and led 4–2 in the fifth. "I remember the changeover at 4–3. I saw my younger brother out of the corner of my eye making signals at me, asking me to fight, not only for myself, but for the rest of the team.

"From that moment, I wasn't thinking anymore. I fought, I ran everywhere, and even if you know that physically you are so tired, you find a new power. When I had won the match I knew I could have played another set because I was so strong mentally. You have to believe that even when you are down, you can still play your best. I was playing really bad before the Davis Cup and look at this.

"We helped each other, even if it was sometimes a subconscious thing. We have one player in the top 100. We're the worst team if you go by the rankings and we have survived in the World Group. That says something about the strength of the character in Belgian tennis. For not such good players, this is definitely the experience of the year."

His brother—who went on to win his first ATP title in Palermo later that year and reflected that it was a direct consequence of his Davis Cup experiences—could only echo those sentiments. "I would say that Davis Cup is the first, better than even the Grand Slams," said Olivier. "It's the only time in the year when your coach is next to you, when your friends are there behind you. The feelings of comradeship are so wonderful.

"This is so important for Belgian tennis because we are the second sport to football and in football we're struggling a little at the moment. It is so important for us to have these moments. Our dream is to have three players in Belgium in the top 50 and we have a good generation with Christophe, who is my best friend as well as my brother, Xavier Malisse, and myself. Tom [Van Houdt] also played great against Italy. There is real hope for Belgian tennis."

The Italians, meantime, were left to wallow in their fate. "And unlike Britain who have Henman and Rusedski, two top quality players," said Rino Tommasi. "We wonder when we are ever going to get back in the World Group again."

FRENCH WHITEWASH

France had had its share of glories and gaffes across the years, but the rollercoaster had been in full motion in the late nineties. From the loss at home in the 1999 Final to the defeat in the first round of the 2000 World Group in Brazil, it was a tortuous journey of disappointment for the French. Their preparation for the tie against Austria, in which defeat would have spelled World Group Final to Euro/African Zone One in six months, was not helped by a wrist injury to their most experienced player, Cedric Pioline.

The pressure was back on Captain Guy Forget. He knew it might be extremely difficult, given the fickle nature of the French tennis public, to survive defeat to a nation that hadn't found anyone yet to fill the shoes of their clay-court master, Thomas Muster. Stefan Koubek had the same blond hair and was a leftie like the former world number 1, but his days of world dominance were a long way off. The leading Austrian, Markus Hipfl, was absent due to injury.

Thus, the Austrians had to rely on a relatively unknown teenager, Jurgen Melzer, in the opening singles against Nicolas Escude, who can blow hot, variable, or cold on court, as the mood took him. His thin face, long nose, and fluffy goatee beard simply added to his mercurial reputation.

On the right day, Escude can be a fearsome opponent, as his 1998 Australian Open semifinal finish indicated. He had ended 1999 with a 15–5 record in his last six tournaments, after struggling for any semblance of form for the previous six months. Thus, Forget was playing with fire and must have wondered how Escude would react to playing the opening singles in Rennes.

He rested a lot easier once Escude swept the debutant Melzer aside 6–2, 6–4, 6–2, before handing the baton to Sebastien Grosjean, who emphatically trounced Koubek, also in straight sets. "We knew it would be a terrible blow for the reputation of French tennis to go down into Group One," said Grosjean. "1999 had been my first year of Davis Cup and we reached the Final, and it has been wonderful for me to play all the matches from the second round on to Nice. We had expected to beat Australia and have a big party,

so to lose made it very difficult for all of us in the team. We felt that maybe Australia wanted it more than us.

"It was tough to have to play Brazil so soon. We didn't have Pioline against Austria but now is the time perhaps to look ahead to [Arnaud] Di Pasquale, to [Arnaud] Clement, and to [Nicolas] Escude. It is good for the French Federation to have these players.

"The Davis Cup was a dream for me when I was young. I had two ambitions, to win the French Open and play Davis Cup. Now one of those has been accomplished."

Escude teamed with Olivier Delaitre in what would be his farewell to the competition. Their overwhelming success over Julien Knowle and Thomas Strengberger completed an unassailable 3–0 lead for the French in nine sets of tennis.

The victory prevented a case of déjà vu, for it was in 1996 that France lifted Dwight's trophy, only to lose in the 1997 first round and be relegated to zonal play in 1998. Who knows what might be next for the nation that has become preeminent in the world of soccer—the 1998 World champions and the 2000 European champions—and won the Davis Cup twice in the last decade?

SWISS ON A ROLL

The Swiss team was becoming adept at hiding their troubles. The fallout from Marc Rosset's departure from the squad was still lingering at the time of their Qualifying Round against Belarus at St. Gallen. Jakob Hlasek, the Swiss captain, would never see eye to eye with Rosset and had to pin his hopes on the freshmen of his team, Roger Federer—widely tipped as one of the talents of the future—and George Bastl.

Once upon a time the prospect of playing Belarus hardly filled teams with dread, but their two leading players have come a long way in what seems like a short space of time. Max Mirnyi is a more-than-competent doubles player who, as an imposing 6'3" specimen with a ready smile and a mighty all-court game, does not find the ladies difficult to attract. Vladimir Voltchkov started from scratch on Wimbledon's qualifying fields of Roehampton and reached the semifinal of the championships in borrowed tennis gear—the first man to achieve such a feat (a semifinalist from qualifying, not the first to do it in someone else's whites) since John McEnroe in 1977.

Voltchkov is a charmer. The crowd warmed to him, and he gave the men's event a nice lift, but when he ran into Sampras in the semis, we all knew what the outcome would be. Voltchkov had done wonders for his own self-belief, and even Switzerland's bigger guns were not about to underestimate him.

Bastl struck the first blow for the Swiss with a more convincing victory over Mirnyi than anyone might have expected.

"It was a tricky match against Max, whose ranking has improved steadily in the past two years," said Bastl. "We'd had a pretty close match against Australia in the first round, when a lot of people hadn't expected us to get more than a few points. I played Lleyton Hewitt in the first match and though I lost, I had the experience I needed.

"I wasn't scared about stepping up. I was confident against Max. We were at home, we had the choice of surface, and I felt good. I had one break in the first set, and survived a set point to win the second on a tiebreak. That set us up."

The ATP Tour guide indicates that the Swiss pronounce his name BAHS-tul, which, when you consider he was born in Chicago, that city of so many rich and diverse bars, is rather apt. Bastl's father, also George, had been a pro ice hockey player, both in his home country and in the States. It was in his second spell in the Windy City, this time with the Chicago Cougars, that young George was born into a sporting heritage, and his father still coaches him.

After Bastl's straight sets victory, it was the time for Federer to take on Voltchkov. Only two weeks had passed since Voltchkov's exploits at Wimbledon, and exactly the kind of titanic battle the two promised occurred during three-and-a-half exhilarating hours.

The tennis was simply stunning. Voltchkov ran so much of Federer's brilliance down, scampering for all his worth and pulling off shots of a Grand Slam vintage, that when the Swiss emerged with a 4–6, 7–5, 7–6, 5–7, 6–2 victory, he justifiably suggested that it was a crucial moment in his life.

Federer was the new giant of the Alpine nation, but the indication from the Swiss camp was that the door had not been shut completely on Rosset, despite this much-publicized falling-out with Captain Hlasek, a legacy of their time together as Davis Cup teammates. "Marc can come back if he wants," Bastl confirmed. "We have left it up to him. He has been upset with the Federation and the captaincy, and if he comes back that's fine, but we do have a solid group of young players for the future. We have fun together, and the Davis Cup experience is helping us all develop."

That was certainly true of Federer, who was growing into the challenge of shouldering the burden of his nation's expectation. The tie was effectively cleaned up when Federer teamed with Lorenzo Manta to defeat

the powerful Mirnyi/Voltchkov combo 2–6, 7–6, 7–6, 7–6, a result that offered Hlasek the chance to try out Michael Kratochvil. Whether the result matters or not, a 6–0, 6–0 whitewash in your Davis Cup debut is something to regale the grandchildren with in later life and that is going to be Kratochvil's pleasure while the young Belarussian Alexander Shvec does his best to forget it ever happened.

ROMANIANS SILENCE HOME CROWD

Zimbabwe, who had come so close to dousing John McEnroe's first year as the United States Davis Cup captain in sackcloth, now had to steady their listing ship to defeat the Romanians in Harare. On the face of it they had an excellent chance, what with home advantage and the loss to the Romanian side of Adrian Voinea, their second highest ranked player, who was in Italy taking his exams. "Adrian said he wanted to finish his schooling and this was the only date he could do it," said his teammate, Andrei Pavel. "I told him that this was such an important match for us in the World Group. But he has had a tough time in the Davis Cup, losing a match last year against Jan Siemerink of Holland from match point up when we would have qualified to play the USA in the quarterfinals, and it had a negative effect on him.

"We lost that match 3–2 in the end and he felt as though it was all his fault. I know that the Davis Cup can bring you down, especially when you play at home and you do not meet the crowd's expectations. The people expect so much of you. When you go to a tournament the week after, you think, 'There's nothing to this.' But there is so much in Davis Cup that is nowhere else."

The chosen number 2 singles player for Romania, Razvan Sabau, could appreciate that. From the very depths of the men's rankings in 1994, the seventeen-year-old Sabau had come from two sets to love down to defeat Britain's Jeremy Bates on grass in Manchester and set up an improbable victory for his country that pitched the British into Euro/African Zone Group Two.

Sabau had not exactly set the world alight since, but he was a more than decent performer. He only briefly threatened in the opening rubber against Byron Black, losing in four sets to the background of a thunderous tin rattling, dancing troupe of Zimbabweans.

But the home side knew that Pavel, arguably the best natural talent to come out of the country since Ilie Nastase, can be dangerous. "I was playing really good tennis going into the tie. I felt in great shape," said Pavel. "What was happening at the time in Zimbabwe [the elections that returned the president Robert Mugabe by a narrow squeak were reaching an uncomfortable hiatus] was pretty scary, but we stayed in a nice hotel and the people were very friendly toward us."

He continued, "I knew I had a lot of responsibility on my shoulders because Voinea wasn't going to be there, but I felt we had a chance with Sabau at number 2 singles. Even when [Sabau] lost to Byron Black, I sensed that [Kevin] Ullyett was nervous playing me in the second match and I was so solid I really didn't give him much of a chance."

Pavel's straight sets victory over Ullyett would be the prelude to an act of bravado through three days that would establish him as a hero in his home country. The first two sets against the balding Ullyett were tight, but once Pavel had won the second set tiebreak 7–2, he was not going to be stopped. On the middle day, he teamed with Gabriel Trifu to defeat Ullyett and Wayne Black, a pair with far greater Davis Cup nous, 7–5, 6–2, 7–6. Now Zimbabwe had to extricate itself from precisely the corner in which it had had the United States in the opening round: 2–1 down with two singles to play.

In such a perilous position, few countries could call on a player with as much experience as Byron Black, who was just coming off a quarterfinal at Wimbledon, his best-ever Grand Slam. But Zimbabwe reckoned without Pavel in his zone, and his third straight-sets win was the most remarkable of all. A total of sixteen aces cleared the path to a 6–2, 6–4, 6–1 victory that sent Zimbabwe back to the Euro/African Zone from which it had been promoted for the first time in 1997.

Pavel's success established a 20–9 singles record for him in Davis Cup and he was treated to rave reviews in Romania, even though he rarely visits his home country since he lives in Germany when he is not airplane-hopping.

"I just love to play in this competition," said Pavel. "I am a very big patriot. I still go to Romania and the people love me there. We all dream that we can get the country back to where it was in the big times of Nastase and Tiriac. I know how much they have done for Romanian tennis. It was a bit different then because they would win. They would stay in the country for parties, but now you have to leave straight away. I guess it's more professional.

"In Romania we must go step by step. To me, winning in Zimbabwe was special for so many reasons, but I have to pay tribute to their people. At such a difficult time for what was happening in their country, they were always so fair. I didn't really give them much of a chance to be too happy."

SWEDEN UNTROUBLED

Of all the tasks to secure a place in the sixteen-nation World Group for 2001, none looked more treacherous than that facing India in Sweden. Their finest singles player, Leander Paes, was absent due to injury. They had to travel to Bastad to play on clay. Everywhere India looked there was trouble.

Even Sweden, seven times the champion nation, was nowhere near full strength either—Magnus Norman and Thomas Enqvist, their two contemporary success stories, were missing from the tie. They could, however, call on the nineteen-year-old Andreas Vinciguerra, the rising teenage star, and a doubles team of Nicklas Kulti and Mikael Tillstrom that oozed international experience.

As it happened, Tillstrom was required for more than that. Captain Carl-Axel Hageskog, who was showered in champagne when he lifted the trophy for Sweden eighteen months earlier, needed to dig deep into his resources and ask Tillstrom if he would play second singles. The affable Tillstrom duly obliged despite the fact that he hadn't played Davis Cup singles since the opening round of the 1998 campaign, when he was beaten by Karol Kucera of the Slovak Republic, only for Sweden to turn the tie on its head and win 3–2 from 2–0 down.

Of the five teenagers who ended 1999 in the world's top 100, Vinciguerra was ranked 96th, but like Federer, Ferrero, Safin, and Hewitt ahead of him, he had made enormous strides. The cherubic Vinciguerra comes from semi-Italian stock: his father, Guiseppe, is a baker specializing in pizzas; his Swedish mother, Gunilla, teaches primary school in his hometown of Malmo.

It was time for Vinciguerra to step into the ring once occupied by Borg, Wilander, Edberg, and Bjorkman. His response was that of a natural, and his 6–3, 6–1, 6–1 victory over Harsh Mankad helped to inspire Tillstrom to a thumping of Prahlad Srinath for the loss of two fewer games than his young compatriot.

The introduction of the doubles specialist Mahesh Bhupathi to partner Fazaluddin Syed, who was as much a mystery as the pronunciation of his name, gave India a renewed hope. They actually led Tillstrom and Kulti by two sets to one, but the Swedes were not to be denied a place in the World Group after a year in the wilderness, and after their victory, Vinciguerra and Tillstrom won their dead rubbers in straight sets for a 5–0 win. The Swedes were back where they belonged.

DUTCH DELIGHT

So, too, were the Dutch. No country that boasts the richness of their talent—the former Wimbledon champion Richard Krajicek, the equally tall and composed Sjeng Schalken, one of the game's finest doubles exponents Paul Haarhuis, and the elegant leftie Jan Siemerink—should have had to worry too much about a journey to Uzbekistan.

Perhaps Holland's greatest enemy would be complacency—or the prospect of frying under the ferocious temperatures in Tashkent that touched 100 degrees on all three days. It was like playing tennis in a kiln. Getting the tie finished before the sun started to play hallucinatory tricks was the Dutch team's objective. They achieved it perfectly.

Krajicek, not exactly the force on clay as he is on fast or grass courts, defeated Oleg Ogodorov in straight sets. Even more emphatic was Schalken's dismissal of the Uzbek number 1, Vadim Kutsenko, for the loss of

seven games. Once Schalken and Haarhuis had romped through the doubles against Ogodorov and Dmitri Tomashevich, Holland had returned to the World Group in two days without dropping a set. The orange contingent that traveled east to support the Dutch was in full-throated delirium.

Haarhuis was offered the privilege of playing the first reverse singles, and his 6–1, 6–2 victory over Vadim Kutsenko moved him to second place on the Dutch Davis Cup all-time list. First place goes to Henk Timmer, king of tennis in the Netherlands in the 1920s, with a win-loss record of 43–22. At 26–15, Haarhuis was a long way off emulation, but his service to his country is another of those exemplary records of support for the Davis Cup that has punctuated the event's history.

above Richard Krajicek marked his return to the Dutch side by overwhelming Oleg Ogorodov in straight sets.

opposite from left to right Nicklas Kulti and Mikael Tillstrom sealed Sweden's victory over India after Andreas Vinciguerra made a winning debut in the opening rubber. Paul Haarhuis's two victories in Tashkent moved him into second place on the Dutch all-time list.

GIOVANNI LAPENTTI

profile *Giovanni Lapentti* | **birthplace** *Guayaquil, Ecuador* | **birthdate** *1•25•83* | **turned professional** *2001* |
Davis Cup records *singles* 3–3 • *doubles* 1–0

"I COMPLETED MY DREAM OF PLAYING WITH NICO IN THE DAVIS CUP."

It was all he could do to stop flooding the room with tears. His hair was continually being ruffled by his teammates on the dais behind him. And not just any old dais, but the center stage at the All England Club, home of Wimbledon.

Giovanni Lapentti could not believe what he had just done and to be fair, neither could anyone else. A come-from-behind, five-set victory over Arvind Parmar of Great Britain had relegated one of the largest standing Davis Cup nations and secured an unlikely berth for Ecuador in the World Group 2001. The kid was beside himself with emotions.

Images of an overjoyed Giovanni raising his racket in victory were thudding down the computer lines and covering the front pages and television screens in Ecuador following the tiny Andean nation's success. But it was the spectacle of hero-worshipping fans overwhelming their new champion as he returned home that will linger in the minds of most people.

Interest levels in tennis have surged in Ecuador following Giovanni's victory that put his nation back in the World Group after a fifteen-year absence. The Lapentti brothers, Giovanni and Nicolas, have earned themselves major celebrity status. At a recent charity function, the shirt Giovanni wore for his Davis Cup victory was auctioned off for $4,000.

Seventeen-year-old Giovanni, the younger of the two, was ranked only 959th in the world, and his twenty-three-year-old brother was ranked 18th. That their team's triumph came on grass and not on clay, the most commonly found South American playing surface, made the success all the more extraordinary. There is only one grass court in Ecuador, and Giovanni had only a month's experience of playing on it before his victory at the All England Club.

Hundreds of fans swarmed outside the Simon Bolivar International Airport in Guayaquil, Ecuador's principal seaport, to welcome home the Davis Cup winners. At a packed press conference, Giovanni told reporters how, when he was two sets down to the rookie Parmar, he "suddenly felt lit up by something indescribable" and began to play

with a patience and cool-headed mentality that he had never before experienced. "I still cannot believe it. I keep seeing mental images of that game and I cannot define what went through my head. I completed my dream of playing with Nico in the Davis Cup."

Captain Raul Viver said that the victory at the All England Club was a dream come true. "I have found the ideal doubles team to play Davis Cup: the Lapentti brothers are the present and the future of Ecuadorian tennis," he said.

As youngsters, the Lapentti brothers began playing tennis in the grounds of the Guayaquil Club, where their father played basketball. Their first great coach was Andres Gomez, a Wimbledon quarterfinalist in 1984 who defeated Andre Agassi to win the 1990 French Open. At forty, Gomez still is a formidable player on the senior circuit but is considered a clay-court specialist.

Yet the Lapenttis' victory at the All England Club cannot be considered a fluke. In addition to Gomez, Ecuadorian tennis has produced other great champions, notably Pancho "Sneaky" Segura in the 1950s. Victor Hugo Araujo, a leading Ecuadorian sportswriter, says that the potential shown by the Lapenttis confirms that individual sport in his country is far stronger than team games. To prove his point, he cites Jefferson Perez, the Olympic gold medal–winning runner, and a host of other South American champions in everything from swimming to chess. The secret? Long-term planning and investment in young athletes at an early age.

"Some people are comparing it to Andres Gomez winning Roland Garros in 1990," said Nicolas Lapentti of his victory. "It was a very long weekend, and it's tough to watch your little brother being down two sets to love in the decisive match. It's completely different from watching a teammate. After I lost to Tim Henman, I told Giovanni that he was in a situation that a lot of players want to be in and that he should just enjoy it. After the match he said that he'd seen how disappointed I was after losing, and he wanted to win the fifth match for me."

Brotherly love has rarely known such extremes.

FINAL ROUND

HISTORY IN THE MAKING

Juan Carlos Ferrero was wrong. "Sunday will come quietly," he said in the characteristically understated way he has with a foreign tongue. Instead, Sunday, December 10, was to be the day this pencil-slim son of Onteniente surrendered his boyhood. It was the day, too, that Spain shed its status as the nearly country of the Davis Cup.

As an intoxicating combination, these two images, of fearless youth and deep-seated desire, proved too potent for defending champions Australia, the nation that had done more than any other to illuminate the event's first century and be everything that Spain itself wanted to be.

That you reached page 18 of Monday's edition of the Barcelona newspaper *Sport* before there was mention of the city's illustrious football team was a compelling measure of the magnitude of Spain's tennis success. "La conquistaros" screamed the headline on the front. The Conquerors. And so it felt for the country that had dispensed with the old, failed formula and came up with a prototype it believed could usher it to glory. And glorious it was.

Ferrero, named Juan Carlos after the King of Spain, was lifted off his feet and greeted with a warm clasp of hands from the man himself—singularly the most captivating moment of his adolescence. The King strode onto the court at a rapturous Palau Sant Jordi to hug each and every one of his victorious Spanish team. He then walked across to pat the cheek of Australian Lleyton Hewitt as a kind-hearted father would a son.

In that moment, maybe, he hoped to cement a reconciliation between winners and losers— a defining moment in sport that sends a flutter through the hearts of those who have never experienced anything like this before, and that grips at the guts of those who have come so close but not quite made it.

The gesture might also have helped Australia come to terms with the antics of the crowds over the three days of the Final. The Spaniards had received a succession of accusations about their behavior, which had tarnished the atmosphere, if never the achievement.

from left to right Lleyton Hewitt made the best possible start for Australia after fighting back from two sets to one down against Albert Costa, a surprise choice for the opening singles.

previous spread Spanish fans attracted criticism for their over-enthusiastic support during the Final.

Several months earlier, Spanish tennis was in the grips of an internal dispute that made this final banquet taste so much the sweeter. John Newcombe, presiding over his final Davis Cup tie after seven years as captain, would undoubtedly have preferred to see Manuel Santana, his friend and contemporary from the golden era of the sixties, sitting on the wicker chair a few yards from where he was perched for the Final.

Instead Newcombe was confronted with the rotund, jack-in-the-box figure of Javier Duarte, who had helped initiate the downfall of Santana and became the subject of so much of the Final's ire. It should be remembered that Santana had played for Spain on their only two previous visits to the Final—in 1965 and '67 when they had lost to Australian teams blessed by the presence of Roy Emerson, Fred Stolle, and Newk himself. It was hardly surprising that he should twice have been elected to the captaincy. In what turned out to be his last match, Santana had taken Spain to New Zealand in September 1999 for a World Group relegation play-off in which a team shorn of Carlos Moya, Alex Corretja, and Albert Costa, its three pivotal players (Felix Mantilla and Francisco Clavet were the singles picks), came home with a 5–0 triumph. Once the draw had been made for 2000, with a clay court route all the way to the Final, Santana must have believed he had a wonderful opportunity of steering Spain to the Cup.

He was called to meet Agustin Pujol, the president of the Spanish Federation, in Barcelona. "Thinking they wanted to discuss these plans, I flew from Màlaga with all my papers," Santana said. "But the first words the president said to me were, 'You're out.' They never gave me the opportunity to find out why they reached this decision."

Santana was not aware that the leading players and their coaches—Corretja and Duarte; Costa and Moya with Jose Perlas—had put together a plan whereby they would share responsibility. Jordi Vilaro and Juan

Avendano, two other famed Spanish coaches, were drawn into the clique, leaving Santana ostracized.

"I was not angry, just sad and very, very disappointed. It was all a big shock to me," he told a group of British tennis writers. Santana watched Spain's first two ties this year, against Italy and Russia. But the country's greatest player, winner of four Grand Slams and holder of every Davis Cup record for Spain (forty-two ties played, ninety-two wins), was treated like a stranger.

Santana's view became more irate and more personal as the Final came closer, especially when he invited his old friend Newcombe to prepare in Marbella (where he has a famous tennis club). The Spanish team greeted this with suspicion that he was trying to subvert their cause despite Santana publicly stating, "I hope my country wins the Davis Cup for the first time. That is the only honor that I never won, as a player or as a captain."

Support for Santana was widespread if not universal, and he refused to attend despite several overtures from the Spanish Federation. "Everybody wants to know why he won't be at the Final," said Miguel Carrero, tennis writer for the Madrid sports daily *Marca*. "Manolo is the lion and it is because of him they stayed in the World Group this year and got the chance to make the Final. The other coaches were jealous of his success and popularity."

Be that as it may, the Spanish gathered at their team's hotel on the Sunday before the Final in a mood of quiet resolve. Corretja had beaten Hewitt in a round robin match at the Tennis Masters Cup in Lisbon a couple of days before and described his opponent as "a little strange," for his on-court exhortations. It should be remembered that Hewitt humbled Corretja 6-0, 6-0, 6-1 on Centre Court at Melbourne Park in the second round of the Australian Open in January, not a score-line any loser would forget in a hurry.

By Monday night, it emerged that the Spanish technical committee—or G4 as they became known—had decided that Corretja would not play on the opening day's singles, preferring to hold him up their sleeve for the doubles and a potentially critical call-up for the reverse singles, if required.

It was a risky strategy, but Duarte and his team believed that Costa had the measure of Hewitt and they knew better than anyone what made Ferrero tick. Whichever way the singles were drawn—on their respective places in the ATP's Entry List, Hewitt would play Costa and Ferrero would meet Patrick Rafter—Spain could finish the first day at worst, at 1–1. Word of Spain's selection intentions began to seep out from HQ, but it wasn't until the draw was made on a bright and mild Thursday that the rumor became reality.

The Australian team could not have prepared better. Rafter, who talked of possible retirement in Key Biscayne in March, was now free of injury and worry and had spent ten days in Marbella lapping up the sunshine. He had never looked fitter. If Rafter embodied the "mate-i-ness" of the Aussie people, Hewitt's personality and attitude were hewn from its rougher edges. Here was a teenager with quicksilver feet, inordinate courage, and a bloody-minded approach to his sport that forced you to tip your hat to him.

He had won back-to-back titles in Adelaide, Sydney, before the Australian Open. He won at Scottsdale and at London's Queen's Club on grass (where he had defeated the king of the green stuff, Pete Sampras, in the final). He had not lost a "live" Davis Cup singles in 2000 but had been beaten by Costa in the Round of 16 at Roland Garros on red clay. It was this result that had helped swing Spain's coaching panel Costa's way.

In his swansong Davis Cup doubles, Mark Woodforde—fretting all the while he was there that his heavily pregnant wife Erin would give birth and he'd be on the first plane back to Rancho Mirage—would partner

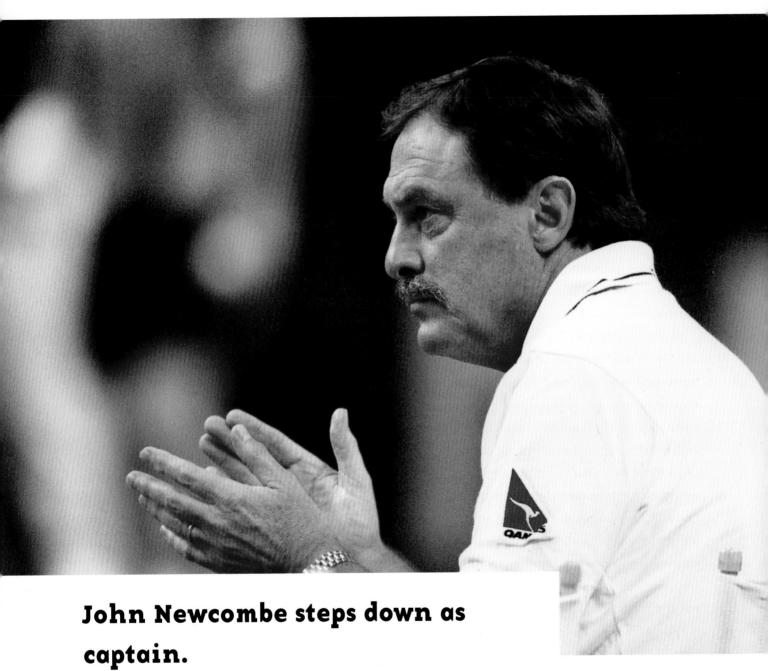

John Newcombe steps down as captain.

above John Newcombe's seven-year term as Australian Davis Cup Captain ended with defeat in Barcelona.

Sandon Stolle, forever known as Son of Fred. The Spaniards would rely on Corretja and Juan Balcells, whose style and build owed nothing to grace.

On the day before the Final, Newcombe reflected on his remarkable passage through this competition: "I first remember 1952 and my dad regaling me with stories of how Frank Sedgman cleaned up the Americans in what was probably going to be his final Davis Cup match. I was eight then. When I was nine, there was the Challenge Round at Kooyong and our wonderful teenagers Lew Hoad and Ken Rosewall beat the Americans (Tony) Trabert and (Vic) Seixas, 3–2 from 2–1 down. I listened to that on the radio, and it finished on a fourth day because of rain. Hoad beat Trabert 7–5 in the fifth and Rosewall took us to victory, beating Seixas in four.

"I was in the stands myself the next year. My dad took me to see the Final at White City in Sydney, where the Americans had vowed revenge. Little did I know that also in the stands that day was a kid called Tony Roche, whose father had brought him up from the bush. We were both having our little private dreams. I pretty much knew there and then that I wanted to play Davis Cup for Australia and if I won Wimbledon too that would be a bonus.

"My first Final was in 1963—I was nineteen. It had become apparent that I was playing really well and that Hop [the legendary Australian coach and captain Harry Hopman] was watching me a fair bit and goading me to see how I responded. He told me at the end of our first week together preparing for the Final that if it was a hot day he would play me and if it wasn't hot he'd play Frase [Neale Fraser]. On the day of the draw, I was standing there fourth in line, still not knowing anything when Hop announced that the singles would be Roy Emerson and John Newcombe. I said to him 'but you didn't say anything to me.' Hop just said: 'I wanted to watch the expression of your face when I read the team out.'

"So, instead of having three days to prepare, to get my nervous system adjusted, I had twenty-four hours. I didn't know if I'd be able to live up to expectations. I went onto court for the first match against Dennis Ralston very nervous and lost the opening set 6–4. I lost the second 6–1 by which time I was getting more nervous. I managed to pull myself to two sets all, but lost it 7–5 in the fifth.

"Then, I played the Wimbledon champion Chuck McKinley in the final rubber, won the first set 12–10, but lost in four. The funny thing is that no one sat down and talked to me afterward, and the media made me out to be a hero even though I lost both matches. It took me about a year to get over it all.

"When I chose Pat Rafter for his first match in '94, the first tie that Tony and I were captain and coach, I spoke to him at length about my first experience and as it turned out, he played two very average matches and was horribly nervous. The next tie was against New Zealand. He was nervous again but we talked him through it and when he won, I told him he would become one of the great Australian players in our Davis Cup history.

"What are my highlights? Of course '63, but ten years on, after I hadn't been allowed to play for five years because I was considered a contract professional in the eyes of the ITF, I was back in the fold and faced the Americans, who had won it each of those years. We were on a mission to get through to the final and put ourselves out of our misery. We thrashed them 5–0 in the Final in Cleveland but I also remember that match for our captain Neale Fraser saying he had to make the most difficult decision of his life and leave Muscles

[Ken Rosewall] out of the doubles to play me and Rod Laver. That was a real hard one for Muscles to swallow.

"In 1976, my last match was at Foro Italico. I played Adriano Panatta in the deciding tie. I finished up losing but I still have a vivid picture of that day in my mind, the things that happened in that match, the crowd. I wanted everything to live on in my memory and it did."

Now, Newcombe had to jolt himself back to the present. His team had been chosen, they had presented themselves in smart attire at the wondrous Palau Generalitat, outside of which stood a rock-garden scene of the Nativity. Stand close to this pretty monument and you'd be doused in a thin drizzle of water sprayed into the air from a dozen minute geysers.

It was a sign for us to wonder at new beginnings. Maybe Spain was on the verge of their birth as a tennis *team*. They had many special players over the years, but they had never been able to gel before. Inside the building, as the speeches dragged on, the eight contestants were sitting alongside each other, trying not to make eye contact.

The focus of attention as the world's media (to be exact three Americans, several Frenchmen, four Italians, six Aussies, a dozen Brits, and someone from every paper in Spain) posed their questions was Spain's decision not to play Corretja on day one. The man himself admitted he had practiced for four days, knowing he was being kept back—when there was a possibility that Spain could be two matches adrift.

"I don't feel I have to play because at their level, Juan Carlos and Albert—they are truly champions," he answered. "They don't need to show anything else to anybody. Our mood is great, we stay calm, we go back to our hotel, listen to music, watch TV, we have created a really good atmosphere.

"There is pressure, but it is there because we feel we have a chance to win. If we were in Australia, playing on grass, there would probably be no pressure. We like the clay, we like Barcelona, we like the situation, now we have to show it out on the court."

Twist his arm and Corretja would admit that he would love to have had the chance to play Hewitt. That might come later. For now, Hewitt was in the spotlight—John Roberts of the British newspaper *The Independent* marked him down as the Ned Kelly of the Aussie team. "The outback outlaw, apart from wearing a bucket over his head, sported a moustache and beard, the growth of which is currently beyond the nineteen-year-old Hewitt, even though the hair on his head extends to a ponytail," Roberts wrote.

None of this would be a consideration except Hewitt's teammates had all grown drip moustaches as a tribute to Newcombe, their hirsute captain. Hewitt couldn't be a "Newk-lookalike." "Unfortunately," said Rafter, "Lleyton is a little bare. Sandon [Stolle] said he'll shave the hair on his bum to put on Lleyton's face." It was the first time anyone had belly-laughed all day.

It was characteristic Aussie humor in face of the odds that had tended to undermine Spain's attempts both to unnerve Hewitt by demonizing him and to engineer a tactical coup by leaving Corretja out. "Perhaps," Newcombe said, "the thinking is that Alex comes in fresh in the doubles and then he'll play the first or second on Sunday, depending on who's won or lost on the Friday. What we have to do is to make it so that it doesn't matter by Sunday."

Corretja seemed at ease with the arrangements, especially if it meant he might get to meet Hewitt in the decisive match on Sunday. "It's going to be a big war to play against each other," he said, "because of the motivation of winning the Davis Cup, and maybe because of our personal situation. What I said about his provocative behavior on the court was my point of view. He's not going to change his personality because I said that. He doesn't have to.

"It's the way he is. I believe the crowd will react against him pretty hard. But still we have to beat him on the court. No matter if they say something to him or whistle at him, he's not going to lose because of that. I think he's going to be pretty pumped."

Hewitt said his reputation as a fire-eater was "maybe something to be proud of." He added: "I'm not worried about it. I've had to deal with a lot of things in such a short career already. I think I've dealt with most of the pressures and stuff that's been put on me pretty well so far." Nor did he seem to be fazed by opening the tie. "Hopefully I can get 1–0 up, and that's going to put a lot of pressure on Juan Carlos coming out 1–0 down, never having played in a Davis Cup Final before."

With that, the press conference was over and Hewitt, eyes on the road ahead, strode roughshod over those radio reporters who wanted a word from him. There were to be no more wasteful incursions on his time—there was work to be done. It was back to the practice court, where he played for two hours on Thursday against hitting partner James Sekulov as if this were the event itself.

The haunting refrain "Bar-ce-lona," the theme for the 1992 Olympic Games sung by Freddie Mercury and Monsarrat Caballe, broke the relative calm of the Palau Sant Jordi at the appointed hour. And the opening ceremony gave some indication of the feelings of the crowd towards the Australians. As Newcombe saluted the section of the stadium where "the Fanatics" were waving their inflatable kangaroos, the jeers rang out, causing the captain to look round wondering if something untoward had happened behind him.

The announcement of each Australian name was similarly greeted. There were none of the expected courtesies. Even Newcombe himself was heckled—not exactly the response he would have expected on his last appearance as the captain. It was going to be a rough three days all around.

For all his self-assurance, Hewitt knew this was going to be something different. He had played the previous year's Final in France, to reasonably limited expectation. Now he was the genuine article, but Australia feared he would not be at his best. Hewitt was still suffering from the effects of a virus picked up in Toronto at the Masters Series back in August. He was 98 percent fit, but the missing 2 percent could be vital in these testing circumstances.

A break point in the opening game came and went, and the moment Costa ripped a forehand down the line to repair the potential damage, the Spaniard let loose, winning the first five games with a succession of dexterously angled forehands that had Hewitt scampering in vain. Costa—supposedly the nontheatrical type—was out-Hewitting Hewitt.

The Australian broke back for 5–2, double-faulted twice in his next game for 30–30, and became involved in a riveting backcourt exchange. He retrieved Costa's extravagant forehand drop shot with one of his own that Costa just managed to get a racket to for a remarkable backhand winner. The crowd erupted. Hewitt was sure the ball had bounced twice but the umpire would have none of it. Set point, saved with an ace; advantage Hewitt. A third ace in the game brought the score to 5–3. The kid had guts, as we already knew.

Newcombe worried more about how much gas Hewitt had in his tank and whether, if he fell behind,

from left to right Australian fans joined Captain John Newcombe in celebrating Lleyton Hewitt's spectacular comeback against Albert Costa.

there was enough deep inside of him to make a real fight of it. Duarte was concerned that Hewitt had chosen the moment Costa stepped up to serve for the set to walk back to his chair and rip the polythene cover from a new racket when nothing seemed wrong with his old one. Duarte bobbed about like a buoy in a storm-tossed sea. Costa, disregarding the sideshow, duly served out to love for a one-set lead.

The second set proved to be a total reversal. On his fifth break point, Hewitt established a 2–0 lead that was doubled to four in the blink of an eye. Costa broke back, but Hewitt responded by taking his serve for the third time and wrapping up the set when, for the first time, Costa made a hash of an attempted drop shot.

Within three games of the third set, Hewitt was changing his racket again, much to the consternation of the Spanish bench. Once more, the timing was bad. Costa had just double-faulted, bringing the score to 40–30, and when he looked back up, Hewitt had his head in his tennis bag for the third time. Duarte couldn't stop himself and tugged at umpire Bruno Rebeuh's trouser leg, making his protest as visible as possible. Newcombe shrugged, as did the umpire. No rule had been broken, but diplomacy wasn't high on Hewitt's agenda.

The games were close—four of the first five went to deuce before Costa stuck his neck in front with a break in the sixth. A further break in the eighth and Costa was two sets to one. Surely there was no way back, not even for this remarkable teenager. But Hewitt broke in the first game of the fourth, and Costa started getting edgy—so much so that when Rebeuh called "let" and the net judge said nothing, Costa had to be pushed back onto the court by his captain.

Another racket change in a Costa service game did little to ease the tension—Duarte was a lighter shade of incandescent—and when Hewitt came out to serve for the set, the noise was louder than it had been the entire match. At 40–30 and set point, Hewitt served a double-fault that was greeted as if it was the winning goal in a World Cup final. He stepped back, drove a winning forehand deep into the corner, and then provoked a wild forehand from Costa into the tramlines. Two sets apiece.

From an all-black garb, Hewitt changed his shirt to red—what more could be done to inflame the bullheads in the Spanish crowd? In the fifth game of the fifth set, Costa was two break points down. He managed to squeak a forehand winner on the first. On the second, Hewitt tried to force a backhand down the line, but it landed an inch wide, causing Hewitt to look across to his bench and shake his head. On a third break point, however, Costa's forehand went long and Hewitt leapt around the court like a dervish.

And so, with no further hitches, the Australian came out to serve for the match and the derision was deafening. Was this fair? Could it be justified? Was there a fair-minded Spaniard in the house? There were tears in the eyes of his mother, Sherilyn. His girlfriend, Belgian player Kim Clijsters, covered her ears. Hewitt netted two straightforward backhands, 0–30. A double-fault, wildly exalted, and it was 0–40. Every time he tossed the ball, they jeered.

Hewitt answered the only way he knew how. An ace made it 15–40; a defensive lob by Costa fell long, 30–40; a weak netted forehand, deuce. Hewitt aced his man again to reach match point, arching his back and letting out a full-throated roar. The roof shook.

The next rally was tortuous. Everyone's eyes were fixed on the ball—crosscourt, down the line, crosscourt again, back and forth—before Hewitt's power down the line drew Costa into a backhand error and the kid collapsed onto his back by the net. A cursory shake of the hand with his opponent and Duarte, and Hewitt rushed to Newcombe, who wrapped him in a bear hug. The Fanatics were going wild, inflatable kangaroos were tossed into the air, and joy abounded. Hewitt had won 3–6, 6–1, 2–6, 6–4, 6–4 in four hours and nine minutes of drama that was made all the more compelling by the conditions through which the young man had fought.

From an hour into Hewitt's match, Rafter had been trying to get his head around the task ahead of him in what might be the last chance he had to get his name inscribed on the old punch bowl. Every time Hewitt fell behind, his heart deflated. Then came his teammate's ultimate glory and Rafter was elated. It was a lot for body and soul to take.

The same, if not more, had to be true of Ferrero, a twenty-year-old of inordinate skills who had dazzled in reaching the semifinal of Roland Garros in May. But this? This was something else. "I am very calm," he said on the day before the Final. "Do not worry about me, I will be fine." One had to admire his sangfroid.

Rafter banged down four first serves in the opening game and won it to love—his tactic was clear. Even though he had been a Parisian semifinalist himself three years earlier and was no puppy on the surface, he didn't want to be out there all night. Ultimately, it was not to be a joyous experience. Ferrero was unshakably calm in the face of such net rushes: picking Rafter off, saving a handful of break points, and extending the opening set into a tiebreak.

When he won the first four points thereof, Ferrero appeared to be strolling, but a couple of rasping service returns and Rafter was right back in it, incredibly winning seven points in a row to pocket the set for himself.

What thoughts were running through those who had chosen the Spanish team? Were four heads about to roll?

Yet, they never doubted Ferrero—not for a minute—and when he held off break points in his first two service games of the second set, one sensed an inexorable turning of the tide. With the first break of serve of the match, he led 4–2, and though Rafter was able to steady himself and hang in for a second tiebreak, once Ferrero was a couple of mini-breaks ahead, he was not to be overhauled.

A love break in the opening game of the third set did everything for Spanish morale. The court seemed to be shrinking from where Rafter stood. He did well not to go 3–0 down in the third, but dropped again to trail 4–1 and had to save two set points in the seventh game. Ferrero was serving for it at 5–2 when, on the opening point, Rafter spun back to smash away, and everything froze.

The cramping was severe and spreading—through his legs, arms, and into his hands. The physio tried to massage some life back into his man and after ten minutes, Rafter was back on his feet. For a few minutes, he was free again, sweeping to three break points, all of which were lost to timid backhands.

Once Ferrero had reasserted himself, winning the third set and leading 3–1 in the fourth, the Aussie knew he had nothing left. His concession was a gracious acceptance of the inevitable.

"He just started to feel it after the second set in his calf muscles and in his right hand which is unusual, because he had never had cramps in those areas before," were Newcombe's first words after a long day had ended 1–1. "We're puzzled. These things are strange. Perhaps it was the tension of Lleyton's match. His body was tensing too much while he was watching it.

"We figured that if his arm was cramping up, with all the problems he's had, he could rehurt his shoulder. It was going to take a miracle for him to come back from that position. It was better to leave it and try to get ready for a fifth match on Sunday, if he's needed."

Of Hewitt's miraculous performance against Costa, the captain paid enormous tribute. "I think it's right up there with the best of them," he said. "We all know that Lleyton hasn't felt that great for the past four months. He went through his own personal pain barrier out there and came out the other side. That's pretty exceptional when you do it under those conditions. But we're only at the end of day one. This is a three-day affair. There's unfinished business to be done."

Newcombe couldn't escape without being reminded of the crowd's behavior and that of his jumpy opposite number. "Lleyton didn't do anything out there to incite the crowd. I thought they were a little unsportsmanlike. He didn't do anything to warrant the treatment he received." When it was suggested to Newk that Duarte had been more cheerleader than coach, he replied: "I think I'll leave that one—it speaks for itself."

Behind the scenes, the Australians were fuming and were about to try to do something about it, but it wasn't until the next day that we learned how upset Newcombe had been. The trigger was defeat in the doubles. Mark Woodforde and Sandon Stolle, a pair with limited experience together, lost in straight sets to the rested Corretja and Juan Balcells in a tie that never really caught fire. Indeed, it was because of the Australians' lack of inspiration that the match suffered mightily. Newcombe chose the aftermath to tear into the crowd.

John Newcombe's final tie as Davis Cup captain was in danger of descending into one of the worst experiences of his life. Australia was on the verge of losing the Cup, and Newcombe accused the Spanish players of inciting the crowd. The Australian had enough experience in six years as captain not to expect to play a Davis Cup Final in cathedral-like quiet, but the constant stream of jeering, whistling, and condemnation directed at his players had eaten away at him to the extent that he couldn't hold back.

"I officially complained before today's match about the crowd and their captain and said I felt a couple of the Spanish players on the bench were inciting the crowd," he said after the doubles defeat left the Australians in the position of needing to win both singles on the final day to retain the Cup.

"I let it go on Friday because it was the first day, but I thought the behavior of the crowd in Lleyton Hewitt's match was disgraceful. I've never been to a match before where every time our boy hit a winner, fourteen thousand people booed. I think their unsportsmanlike behavior has been displayed in front of the world. They might be proud of themselves, but the whole world has been watching this."

The announcement of the names of the Australian doubles team on Saturday was greeted with deafening jeers. What had Mark Woodforde done to offend the people of Spain? Had any of them even laid eyes on Sandon Stolle before? In his first two service games, whistles interrupted Woodforde's ball toss. Newcombe tugged umpire Bruno Rebeuh on the trouser leg and asked him to say something.

After Alex Corretja's serve had been broken to love in the sixth game of the second set, Newcombe swiveled around to the Aussie support group and waved his arms in a manner that appeared to relay the message "We've turned it around." It incensed certain members of the non-playing Spanish bench and caused referee Stefan Fransson to march onto court and pull the two captains together. "He told us both to cut it out," said Newcombe. "Javier said, 'Well if he does, I will.' That's why I burst out laughing, it's just a comedy."

Losing, though, would be no laughing matter. Woodforde and Stolle were no match for Corretja and the bulldozing figure of Juan Balcells, losing 6–4, 6–4, 6–4, in a manner that belied their far greater weight of big-match experience. Woodforde, in his last appearance in an event he has graced for seven years, has won doubles titles all over the world, but even he was dumbfounded at the level of animosity toward him.

"I felt like a caged animal out there," he said. "The crowd was pretty disgraceful. I've never heard a crowd boo or be so unsportsmanlike for any type of winner we hit. I guess it's the way they behave but it was very disappointing to have to be out there living and breathing it. I'm sure as hell if we played in Australia it wouldn't be like that."

Francesco Ricci Bitti, the president of the ITF, was happy to put his views on the record: "I felt a little bit disturbed at the end of the first match on the first day, to have a disturbance between the first and second service," he said. "In trying to defend the situation, I don't think it changed anything in the games. In a great city, my experience is that people are not tennis people. On one side, it is good to get people that are not the usual tennis fans, but there is some danger."

The thought of starting to impose penalties on the crowd did not enter the thinking of the chairman of the Davis Cup committee, the Spaniard Juan Margets. While condemning attempts to disturb Hewitt in the final game of his opening singles, Margets said: "But this is not something to rule on. This is to do with fair sportsmanship. To consider what has been happening here in terms of booing affecting the image of a sport, only in tennis among the really popular global sports is that an issue. This is a conversation that would not take place in football, basketball, et cetera."

But it did not make it right for tennis, either. For all that, the Swedish referee Stefan Fransson stressed to his two umpires, Mike Morrissey of England and Bruno Rebeuh of France, to be tougher on the last day.

And so the scene was set for the final day with Spain in the driving seat. A midday announcement confirmed the speculation that Duarte would leave Ferrero in the firing line against Hewitt, and select Corretja instead of Costa to meet Rafter in the potentially decisive fifth rubber. But the suggestion that it may all hinge on the last match between Corretja and Rafter rather overlooked the confidence coursing through the ice-cool veins of young Ferrero.

The final day of the Final was given royal assent. King Juan Carlos and Queen Sofia were in attendance, seated next to Juan Antonio Samaranch, who will retire as president of the International Olympic Committee next year. Their gold-tinted eyes, plus those of fourteen thousand more demonstrative natives, were focused on who had finished the year ranked 12th in the Champions Race. Hewitt was the demon figure again.

The clash proved to be a classic completion to the year. The opening was crazy enough, with two immediate breaks of serve by Ferrero. He broke again in the fifth game and again in the seventh to win the opening set in thirty-five minutes. Once more, it seemed, Hewitt was trying to conserve too much; he was going to have to open out. At the completion of the first set, Duarte dashed off behind the black awning draping the court, and one wondered if he was telling Corretja not to drive himself into the ground on the practice court, the boy was doing just fine. Then, Hewitt awoke, as if from forty winks. The first fist pump and "C'mon!" roused the Australian and his support group, but Ferrero saved the three break points in the second game of the set and immediately broke to lead 2–1. It should have been 4–1, but a net cord went Hewitt's way and he followed it up with a blistering forehand winner. It was 3–2 instead, and hope sprang eternal.

A decisive time was upon us. Hewitt broke back to level the set at 4–4. He was able to withstand a break point for 6–5 with three successive drilled groundstrokes that swept the lines, and then found himself with two set points to square the match. Where he had hardly missed a groundie from the baseline all day, Hewitt suddenly contrived to slash at two routine shots, one backhand, the next a forehand. Ferrero was back in it, but it was hardly of his own doing.

The tiebreak went Ferrero's way, courtesy of one netted backhand on set point. The third set went to Hewitt thanks to a single break of serve. It was time to draw breath, for Ferrero was serving first in a set that, if he won it, would secure the Davis Cup for Spain.

The nerves were jangling. Hewitt saved a break point with a broken string (this time Duarte could have no complaints about an equipment change), but in the next game, the Aussie was involved in a verbal exchange with leading British umpire Mike Morrissey, whom he had summoned from his chair to check a mark on the sideline. Morrissey ruled in Ferrero's favor, and Hewitt balked. The two discussed the decision, and it was not until Morrissey asked Newcombe to have a word with his man that tempers cooled. Three games later, when a Hewitt serve that brushed the line was called out and Morrissey rightly called "first serve," it was all Newcombe could do to persuade Hewitt to continue playing.

Hewitt contrived to lose that game and we assumed it was a decisive loss, for Ferrero was now serving for the Davis Cup. But he rushed every shot, lost it to 15, and Duarte was signaling for the first time for his boy to keep his head. The next moment, the captain was pushing his man out to receive serve—maybe the Australian would finally weaken.

At 15–40, with two points for the Cup, an eerie hush descended. Ferrero netted a backhand to 30–40; then he tried to smack an inside-out forehand down the middle and found the lowest part of the net. Deuce. Hewitt double-faulted, but this time the reaction was not quite as heated as it had been on Friday. Ferrero's forehand flew wide after another breathtaking rally. How would it end?

Spain went to match point number four after a brilliant forehand crosscourt winner—this time, surely! These two kids—we should not forget how little experience they have—traded baseline punches until Hewitt went crosscourt and Ferrero, summoning every nerve in his body, produced the picture-perfect backhand winner down the line.

He sank to his knees, fell onto his back, and the next few minutes were lost as Duarte leapt on top of him—not something to be recommended—and the rest of the Spanish contingent followed en masse. Hewitt shook the umpire's hand, took Newcombe's, and was in the dressing room before Ferrero had staggered back to his feet.

And so the blond boy king of Spanish tennis was swept off his feet to meet the King himself, and in celebration of the moment he delivered the bauble they had waited sixty-five years to raise. Ferrero was carried on the shoulders of Alex Corretja to his blue-blooded namesake who leaned down from the front row of the VIP box to shake the hands that had finally grasped the coveted Davis Cup.

He had the expression of a kid not exactly sure of what he had done. Being acclaimed a conquering hero was a bit too much for him, but he rose to the occasion and carried the Palau Sant Jordi around like a matador at a kill. It probably felt like he had tweaked a bull by the tail, for his 6–2, 7–6, 4–6, 6–4 victory over Hewitt spanned three hours and forty-seven minutes of emotion-charged tennis, most of the time spent trading brilliance and brawn from the baseline.

"It's hard to take," said Hewitt, "especially being the one out there to lose the Davis Cup. Two days ago I was saying I'd had my best experience ever on a tennis court and now I'm going through my worst. I was on top of the world coming back from two sets to one down to win. How things change so quickly. I gave everything I had in both matches. I couldn't have done any more for myself or for the team. To his credit, he came up with the big points at the big moments. It's tough to stop someone in that situation.

"I wanted to give Pat the fifth match. It was hard to be out there with a silver medal around my neck, that's for sure."

I said to Duarte afterwards that we were a bit concerned when he ran onto the court and leapt on Ferrero that the boy would not get up again. "That is your first funny question for three days," he replied, to Spanish laughter. "No, Juan Carlos carried the game very, very well, and the last points were just marvelous. He played marvelous."

Ferrero was asked if the win would change his life. "It's definitely a great, great experience for the future and other tournaments," he replied. "I need to take the profit from this and I am only twenty. The future is everything now."

No, Juan Carlos, this was no quiet Sunday. It was the loudest you might ever have in your life.

JUAN CARLOS FERRERO

profile *Juan Carlos Ferrero* | birthplace *Onteniente, Spain* | birthdate 2•12•80 | turned professional 1998 |

Davis Cup records *singles* 5–0 • *doubles* 0–0

"I THINK IT'S GOING TO BE FUN TO BE FAMOUS."

He is known as the Mosquito. Try swatting him away and he becomes even more aggressive. With his blond hair, all-black outfit, and purple-stringed racquet, Ferrero is making the vivid splashes of color across men's tennis that compatriot Sergio Garcia made in golf and goalkeeper Iker Casillas made in the Real Madrid club's return to European prominence.

These trendy ninos are at the forefront of a Spanish sporting renaissance. But while the footballers and golfers of that passionate country have enjoyed a garlanded place in the hearts and minds of the public, the reaction to their tennis players has, for the most part, been strictly small print.

Manuel Santana's Wimbledon victory the same summer England won the World Cup inspired a generation of Brits to change their holiday destinations and seek out the beaches of the Costa Brava. Since Santana's graceful game earned him three Grand Slam championships in the mid-sixties, Manuel Orantes and Andres Gimeno flirted with fame until Sergei Bruguera burst to prominence at Roland Garros in 1993.

The mantle was passed to Carlos Moya, the 1998 French Open champion and briefly world number 1 last year, and Alex Corretja, who came back from two sets to love down to beat Moya and win the ATP Tour World championship in 1998, rising to number 3 in the world the same year.

Now Ferrero is the lauded one. At a glitzy celebration at the Monte Carlo Sporting Club in April, the twenty-year-old was acclaimed as the ATP Tour Newcomer of the Year, joining a distinguished cast that includes the late Vitas Gerulaitus, John McEnroe, Patrick Rafter, and Mark Philippoussis.

Bad days have been few and far between for Chavalito (the "little kid") since he broke into the world's top 100 in 1999 and won his first tour title in a converted bull-ring in Mallorca. It was only a matter of time before he was elected to his country's Davis Cup team,

walloping Yevgeny Kafelnikov, the Russian former world number 1, in straight sets to cement Spain's place in the 2000 semifinals.

"Last year, I was the promise. Now I am the reality," said Ferrero. "I would like everyone in Spain and the world to know that I am a strong competitor."

There is nothing of Santana's grace in Ferrero's game; indeed, he is very much in the Spanish vogue, pounding the ball with virulent topspin on the forehand and playing double-fisted on the backhand. "I play very fast, very physical. The Davis Cup was a fantastic experience for me. I expected to be nervous, but I slept very well the night before. Six thousand people in the stadium were supporting me and it felt so good, so different. I think it's going to be fun to be famous."

Ferrero uses his successes to pay tribute to his mother, Rosario, who died from breast cancer four years ago. "When I won my first tournament in Majorca I sent a kiss in the sky to my mother," he said. "It was the same after I won in Davis Cup, one kiss for her. I play for her all the time."

Ferrero was within one step of the Roland Garros final before defeat in the semis to Gustavo Kuerten. On the way, he had shaken several leading stars to their roots, notably Philippoussis and, in the quarters, his compatriot and surrogate brother, Corretja.

Corretja is full of admiration: "The good thing is, he is an even better guy than he is a player, and that is really important. He has many things to learn, but he is going to be good on every surface, believe me. I can see that Juan Carlos and Lleyton Hewitt are going to be the best guys on the tour. They are both great talents. It is only a matter of time before Juan Carlos wins something really big."

Little did Corretja know that his words in the spring would come true on a never-to-be-forgotten Sunday afternoon in Barcelona in December, when the kid took flight on the wings of greatness.

RESULTS

WORLD GROUP

USA defeated Zimbabwe 3–2, Harare ZIM; Hard (I)
Andre Agassi USA d. Wayne Black ZIM 7–5 6–3 7–5 | *Byron Black* ZIM d. Chris Woodruff USA 7–6(2) 6–3 6–2 | *Wayne Black/Kevin Ullyett* ZIM d. Rick Leach/Alex O'Brien USA 7–6(4) 5–7 0–6 7–5 7–5 | *Andre Agassi* USA d. Byron Black ZIM 6–2 6–3 7–6(4) | *Chris Woodruff* USA d. Wayne Black ZIM 6–3 6–7(2) 6–2 6–4

Czech Republic defeated Great Britain 4–1, Ostrava CZE Clay (I)
Tim Henman GBR d. Slava Dosedel CZE 6–7(4) 5–7 6–1 7–5 6–3 | *Jiri Novak* CZE d. Jamie Delgado GBR 6–4 7–6(4) 6–3 | *Jiri Novak/David Rikl* CZE d. Neil Broad/Tim Henman GBR 7–6(4) 6–4 6–7(4) 6–2 | *Jiri Novak* CZE d. Tim Henman GBR 6–4 6–2 6–2 | *Bohdan Ulihrach* CZE d. Jamie Delgado GBR 5–7 7–5 6–4

Spain defeated Italy 4–1, Murcia ESP; Clay (O)
Albert Costa ESP d. Davide Sanguinetti ITA 6–4 6–4 6–2 | *Alex Corret.ja* ESP d. Andrea Gaudenzi ITA 4–6 6–1 6–1 6–1 | *Juan Balcells/Alex Corret.ja* ESP d. Andrea Gaudenzi/Diego Nargiso ITA 6–3 6–4 6–1 | *Andrea Gaudenzi* ITA d. Albert Costa ESP 5–7 7–5 6–4 | *Francisco Clavet* ESP d. Vincenzo Santopadre ITA 6–7(5) 6–1 6–3

Russia defeated Belgium 4–1, Moscow RUS; Carpet (I)
Yevgeny Kafelnikov RUS d. Filip Dewulf BEL 6–7(3) 6–4 7–5 6–2 | *Marat Safin* RUS d. Christophe Rochus BEL 7–5 3–6 6–2 6–4 | *Andrei Cherkasov/Marat Safin* RUS d. Christophe Rochus/Olivier Rochus BEL 4–6 7–6(2) 1–6 6–1 6–3 | *Mikhail Youzhny* RUS d. Olivier Rochus BEL 7–6(6) 6–2 | *Filip Dewulf* BEL d. Andrei Cherkasov RUS 6–0 4–6 6–1

Slovak Republic defeated Austria 3–2, Bratislava SVK; Carpet (I)
Karol Kucera SVK d. Markus Hipfl AUT 6–2 6–3 6–3 | *Dominik Hrbaty* SVK d. Stefan Koubek AUT 6–4 6–4 6–4 | *Dominik Hrbaty/Karol Kucera* SVK d. Julian Knowle/Alexander Peya AUT 6–4 6–3 6–4 | *Stefan Koubek* AUT d. Jan Kroslak SVK 6–3 6–2 | *Markus Hipfl* AUT d. Ladislav Svarc SVK 6–2 6–4

Brazil defeated France 4–1, Florianopolis BRA; Clay (O)
Fernando Meligeni BRA d. Cedric Pioline FRA 7–5 5–7 4–6 6–1 6–4 | *Gustavo Kuerten* BRA d. Jerome Golmard FRA 6–3 3–6 6–3 6–2 | *Gustavo Kuerten/Jaime Oncins* BRA d. Nicolas Escude/Cedric Pioline FRA 6–4 6–4 6–4 | *Nicolas Escude* FRA d. Gustavo Kuerten BRA 6–2 7–6(3) | *Francisco Costa* BRA d. Arnaud Clement FRA 7–6(5) 5–7 6–2

Germany defeated Netherlands 4–1, Leipzig GER; Carpet (I)
Tommy Haas GER d. John Van Lottum NED 4–6 7–6(4) 6–3 6–2 | *Sjeng Schalken* NED d. Rainer Schuttler GER 3–6 7–6(2) 6–1 6–0 | *Marc-Kevin Goellner/David Prinosil* GER d. Paul Haarbuis/Jan Siemerink NED 4–6 6–3 7–6(3) 6–3 | *Tommy Haas* GER d. Sjeng Schalken NED 6–2 6–2 6–3 | *David Prinosil* GER d. John Van Lottum NED 6–3 6–3

Australia defeated Switzerland 3–2, Zurich SUI; Hard (I)
Lleyton Hewitt AUS d. George Bastl SUI 4–6 6–3 6–2 6–4 | *Roger Federer* SUI d. Mark Philippoussis AUS 6–4 7–6(3) 4–6 6–4 | *Roger Federer/Lorenzo Manta* SUI d. Wayne Arthurs/Sandon Stolle AUS 3–6 6–3 6–4 7–6(4) | *Lleyton Hewitt* AUS d. Roger Federer SUI 6–2 3–6 7–6(2) 6–1 | *Mark Philippoussis* AUS d. George Bastl SUI 6–7(3) 6–4 3–6 6–3 6–4

USA defeated Czech Republic 3–2, Inglewood, CA USA; Carpet (I)
Jiri Novak CZE d. Pete Sampras USA 7–6(1) 6–3 6–2 | *Andre Agassi* USA d. Slava Dosedel CZE 6–3 6–3 6–3 | *Jiri Novak/David Rikl* CZE d. Alex OíBrien/Jared Palmer USA 7–5 6–4 6–4 | *Andre Agassi* USA d. Jiri Novak CZE 6–3 6–3 6–1 | *Pete Sampras* USA d. Slava Dosedel CZE 6–4 6–4 7–6(2)

Spain defeated Russia 4–1, Malaga ESP; Clay (O)
Alex Corret.ja ESP d. Marat Safin RUS 6–4 6–3 5–7 6–1 | *Juan Carlos Ferrero* ESP d. Yevgeny Kafelnikov RUS 6–2 6–2 6–2 | *Yevgeny Kafelnikov/Marat Safin* RUS d. Juan Balcells/Alex Corretja ESP 7–6(4) 2–6 7–6(3) 6–4 | *Albert Costa* ESP d. Yevgeny Kafelnikov RUS 6–0 6–3 6–0 | *Juan Carlos Ferrero* ESP d. Marat Safin RUS 6–0 6–3

Brazil defeated Slovak Republic 3–2, Rio de Janeiro BRA; Clay (O)
Dominik Hrbaty SVK d. Fernando Meligeni BRA 6–1 7–5 6–2 | *Gustavo Kuerten* BRA d. Karol Kucera SVK 2–6 6–3 4–6 7–5 6–1 | *Gustavo Kuerten/Jaime Oncins* BRA d. Dominik Hrbaty/Karol Kucera SVK 6–3 2–6 6–2 6–3 | *Dominik Hrbaty* SVK d. Gustavo Kuerten BRA 7–5 6–4 7–6(5) | *Fernando Meligeni* BRA d. Karol Kucera SVK 5–7 7–6(6) 6–2 6–4

Australia defeated Germany 3–2, Adelaide AUS; Grass (O)
Lleyton Hewitt AUS d. Michael Kohlmann GER 6–1 6–1 6–2 | *Wayne Arthurs* AUS d. David Prinosil GER 7–6(4) 3–6 7–6(3) 6–7(7) 11–9 | *Patrick Rafter/Mark Woodforde* AUS d. Marc-Kevin Goellner/David Prinosil GER 6–3 6–2 2–6 6–7(4) 10–8 | *Rainer Schuttler* GER d. Lleyton Hewitt AUS 26 6–3 6–4 | *Michael Kohlmann* GER d. Wayne Arthurs AUS 7–5 7–6(5)

Australia defeated Brazil 5–0, Brisbane AUS; Grass (O)
Patrick Rafter AUS d. Gustavo Kuerten BRA 6–3 6–2 6–3 | *Lleyton Hewitt* AUS d. Fernando Meligeni BRA 6–4 6–2 6–3 | *Sandon Stolle/Mark Woodforde* AUS d. Gustavo Kuerten/Jaime Oncins BRA 6–7(3) 6–4 3–6 6–3 6–4 | *Lleyton Hewitt* AUS d. Andre Sa BRA 6–4 6–1 | *Patrick Rafter* AUS d. Fernando Meligeni BRA 6–3 6–4

Spain defeated USA 5–0, Santander ESP; Clay (O)
Albert Costa ESP d. Todd Martin USA 6–4 6–4 6–4 | *Alex Corret.ja* ESP d. Jan Michael Gambill USA 1–6 6–3 6–4 6–4 | *Juan Balcells/Alex Corret.ja* ESP d. Todd Martin/Chris Woodruff USA 7–6(6) 2–6 6–3 6–7(5) 6–3 | *Juan Carlos Ferrero* ESP d. Vince Spadea USA 4–6 6–1 6–4 | *Juan Balcells* (ESP d. Jan Michael Gambill USA 1–6 7–6(2) 6–4

Spain defeated Australia 3–1, Barcelona ESP; Clay (I)
Lleyton Hewitt AUS d. Albert Costa ESP 3–6 6–1 2–6 6–4 6–4 | *Juan Carlos Ferrero* ESP d. Patrick Rafter AUS 6–7(4) 7–6(2) 6–2 3–1 ret. | *Juan Barcells/Alex Corret.ja* ESP d. Sandon Stolle/Mark Woodforde AUS 6–4 6–4 6–4 | *Juan Carlos Ferrero* ESP d. Lleyton Hewitt AUS 6–2 7–6(5) 4–6 6–4 | *Alex Corretja* ESP v Patrick Rafter AUS–not played

QUALIFYING ROUND FOR THE 2001 WORLD GROUP

Ecuador defeated Great Britain 3–2, London GBR; Grass (O)
Nicolas Lapentti ECU d. Greg Rusedski GBR 6–3 6–7(3) 7–5 4–6 7–5 | *Tim Henman* GBR d. Luis Morejon ECU 6–2 6–1 6–4 | *Giovanni Lapentti/Nicolas Lapentti* ECU d. Tim Henman/Arvind Parmar GBR 6–3 7–5 6–3 | *Tim Henman* GBR d. Nicolas Lapentti ECU 6–1 6–4 6–4 | *Giovanni Lapentti* ECU d. Arvind Parmar GBR 4–6 3–6 6–1 6–3 6–3

Romania defeated Zimbabwe 3–2, Harare ZIM; Hard (I)
Byron Black ZIM d. Razvan Sabau ROM 6–2 4–6 7–5 6–2 | *Andrei Pavel* ROM d. Kevin Ullyett ZIM 6–4 7–6(2) 6–2 | *Andrei Pavel/Gabriel Trifu* ROM d. Wayne Black/Kevin Ullyett ZIM 7–5 6–2 7–6(2) | *Andrei Pavel* ROM d. Byron Black ZIM 6–2 6–4 6–1 | *Wayne Black* ZIM d. Razvan Sabau ROM 6–3 7–6(2)

Netherlands defeated Uzbekistan 4–1, Tashkent UZB; Clay (O)
Richard Krajicek NED d. Oleg Ogorodov UZB 6–4 6–3 6–4 | *Sjeng Schalken* NED d. Vadim Kutsenko UZB 6–2 6–1 6–4 | *Paul Haarbuis/Sjeng Schalken* NED d. Oleg Ogorodov/Dmitri Tomashevich UZB 6–3 6–1 7–6(0) | *Paul Haarbuis* NED d. Vadim Kutsenko UZB 6–1 6–2 | *Oleg Ogorodov* UZB d. Sjeng Schalken NED 6–4 6–3

France defeated Austria 5–0, Rennes FRA; Carpet (I)
Nicolas Escude FRA d. Jurgen Melzer AUT 6–2 6–4 6–2 | *Sebastien Grosjean* FRA d. Stefan Koubek AUT 6–3 6–2 6–3 | *Olivier Delaitre/Nicolas Escude* FRA d. Julian Knowle/Thomas Strengberger AUT 6–4 6–3 6–3 | *Jerome Golmard* FRA d. Stefan Koubek AUT 6–4 6–4 | *Sebastien Grosjean* FRA d. Jurgen Melzer AUT 3–6 6–3 7–5

Sweden defeated India 5–0, Bastad SWE; Clay (O)
Andreas Vinciguerra SWE d. Harsh Mankad IND 6–3 6–1 6–1 | *Mikael Tillstrom* SWE d. Prahlad Srinath IND 6–2 6–0 6–1 | *Nicklas Kulti/Mikael Tillstrom* SWE d. Mahesh Bhupathi/Fazaluddin Syed IND 6–3 3–6 4–6 6–3 6–3 | *Andreas Vinciguerra* SWE d. Prahlad Srinath IND 6–2 6–1 | *Mikael Tillstrom* SWE d. Harsh Mankad IND 6–3 6–0

Belgium defeated Italy 4–1, Mestre Venezia ITA; Clay (O)

Olivier Rochus BEL d. *Andrea Gaudenzi* ITA 6–2 7–5 6–3 | *Davide Sanguinetti* ITA d. *Filip Dewulf* BEL 1–6 7–6(5) 7–5 6–0 | *Christophe Rochus/Tom Van Houdt* BEL d. *Andrea Gaudenzi/Diego Nargiso* ITA 6–4 6–4 6–4 | *Christophe Rochus* BEL d. *Davide Sanguinetti* ITA 6–2 7–5 6–7(6) 1–6 7–5 | *Filip Dewulf* BEL d. *Renzo Furlan* ITA 7–5 6–2

Switzerland defeated Belarus 5–0, St Gallen SUI; Hard (I)

George Bastl SUI d. *Max Mirnyi* BLR 6–4 7–6(4) 6–2 | *Roger Federer* SUI d. *Vladimir Voltchkov* BLR 4–6 7–5 7–6(1) 5–7 6–2 | *Roger Federer/Lorenzo Manta* SUI d. *Max Mirnyi/Vladimir Voltchkov* BLR 2–6 7–6(5) 7–5 7–6(4) | *Michel Kratochvil* SUI d. *Alexander Shvec* BLR 6–0 6–0 | *Lorenzo Manta* SUI d. *Vassili Kajera* BLR 7–6(0) 6–1 | The winners of these seven ties, along with Morocco, qualified for the World Group in 2001. The losers remained in, or were relegated to, their respective Group I Zones in 2001

GROUP I

Euro/African Zone, First Round • 4–6 February

Ukraine defeated Portugal 4–1, Kiev UKR; Carpet (I)

Andrey Dernovskiy UKR d. *Joao Cunha-Silva* POR 7–6(6) 6–4 3–6 3–6 6–4 | *Andrei Medvedev* UKR d. *Bernardo Mota* POR 6–1 6–3 4–6 6–2 | *Andrei Medvedev/Andrei Rybalko* UKR d. *Emanuel Couto/Joao Cunha-Silva* POR 7–5 6–4 6–4 | *Orest Tereshchuk* UKR d. *Joao Cunha-Silva* POR 6–3 6–4 | *Bernardo Mota* POR d. *Andrey Dernovskiy* UKR 7–5 3–6 7–6(5)

Second Round • 7–9 April

Sweden defeated Finland 3–2, Helsinki FIN; Hard (I)

Magnus Norman SWE d. *Ville Liukko* FIN 6–3 4–6 6–1 7–6(7) | *Tuomas Ketola* FIN d. *Mikael Tillstrom* SWE 6–3 3–6 4–6 6–4 6–3 | *Nicklas Kulti/Mikael Tillstrom* SWE d. *Tuomas Ketola/Ville Liukko* FIN 6–1 6–1 6–4 | *Magnus Norman* SWE d. *Tuomas Ketola* FIN 6–2 6–4 6–1 | *Jarkko Nieminen* FIN d. *Mikael Tillstrom* SWE 6–1 6–4

Romania defeated Hungary 3–2, Bucharest HUN; Hard (I)

Andrei Pavel ROM d. *Gergely Kisgyorgy* HUN 6–2 7–6(5) 5–7 6–7(8) 6–2 | *Attila Savolt* HUN d. *Razvan Sabau* ROM 6–4 6–3 6–2 | *Gabor Koves/Attila Savolt* HUN d. *Dinu Pescariu/Gabriel Trifu* ROM 6–1 5–7 6–3 3–6 7–5 | *Andrei Pavel* ROM d. *Attila Savolt* HUN 6–4 1–6 6–4 6–2 | *Dinu Pescariu* ROM d. *Gergely Kisgyorgy* HUN 6–3 7–5 6–7(3) 6–4

Belarus defeated South Africa 4–1, Belarus BLR; Carpet (I)

Vladimir Voltchkov BLR d. *Neville Godwin* RSA 6–2 7–6(2) 7–5 | *Max Mirnyi* BLR d. *Jeff Coetzee* RSA 6–3 6–2 6–4 | *David Adams/John-Laffnie De Jager* RSA d. *Sergei Samoseiko/Alexander Shvec* BLR 7–6(2) 6–1 6–3 | *Max Mirnyi* BLR d. *Neville Godwin* RSA 6–4 6–3 6–4 | *Vladimir Voltchkov* BLR d. *Jeff Coetzee* RSA 6–1 6–2

Morocco defeated Ukraine 3–2, Casablanca MAR; Clay (O)

Andrei Medvedev UKR d. *Hicham Arazi* MAR 6–4 1–6 6–2 3–6 7–5 | *Younes El Aynaoui* MAR d. *Andrey Dernovskiy* UKR 6–2 6–2 6–3 | *Karim Alami/Hicham Arazi* MAR d. *Andrei Medvedev/Andrei Rybalko* UKR 3–6 6–1 7–5 6–3 | *Andrei Medvedev* UKR d. *Younes El Aynaoui* MAR 7–5 7–5 6–2 | *Hicham Arazi* MAR d. *Orest Tereshchuk* UKR 6–4 6–0 6–1 | Sweden, Romania, Belarus and Morocco qualified for World Group Qualifying Round

3rd Round/Playoff • 6–8 October

Finland defeated Hungary 4–1, Helsinki FIN; Carpet (I)

Ville Liukko FIN d. *Gergely Kisgyorgy* HUN 6–1 6–3 6–3 | *Jarkko Nieminen* FIN d. *Attila Savolt* HUN 6–2 1–6 7–6(5) 6–0 | *Gabor Koves/Attila Savolt* HUN d. *Tuomas Ketola/Ville Liukko* FIN 4–6 7–6(5) 6–4 7–5 | *Ville Liukko* FIN d. *Attila Savolt* HUN 2–6 5–7 6–4 6–4 6–4 | *Jarkko Nieminen* FIN d. *Gergely Kisgyorgy* HUN 6–3 6–2

Portugal defeated South Africa 3–2, Maia POR; Clay (O)

Bernardo Mota POR d. *Justin Bower* RSA 6–4 6–1 7–5 | *Wayne Ferreira* RSA d. *Emanuel Couto* POR 6–1 6–4 6–4 | *Emanuel Couto/Nuno Marques* POR d. *John-Laffnie De Jager/Piet Norval* RSA 4–6 7–6(7) 6–3 3–6 8–6 | *Wayne Ferreira* RSA d. *Bernardo Mota* POR 6–3 6–2 4–6 6–3 | *Emanuel Couto* POR d. *Justin Bower* RSA 7–6(4) 4–6 4–6 7–6(6) 6–4 | Hungary and South Africa relegated to Euro/African Zone Group II in 2001

American Zone, First Round • 4–6 February

Chile defeated Canada 4–1, Vina Del Mar CHI; Clay (O)

Fernando Gonzalez CHI d. *Sebastien Lareau* CAN 2–6 6–3 1–6 6–2 6–1 | *Nicolas Massu* CHI d. *Simon Larose* CAN 6–0 6–7(2) 3–1 ret. | *Fernando Gonzalez/Nicolas Massu* CHI d. *Sebastien Lareau/Jocelyn Robichaud*

CAN 6–4 6–4 2–6 6–2 | *Frederic Niemeyer* CAN d. *Adrian Garcia* CHI 4–6 6–1 7–6(6) | *Hermes Gamonal* CHI d. *Simon Larose* CAN 6–2 7–5

Ecuador defeated Colombia 5–0, Bogota COL; Clay (O)

Luis Morejon ECU d. *Eduardo Rincon* COL 2–6 7–5 7–5 2–6 6–0 | *Nicolas Lapentti* ECU d. *Pablo Gonzalez* COL 4–6 6–4 7–6(12) 7–6(3) | *Andres Gomez/Nicolas Lapentti* ECU d. *Pablo Gonzalez/Ruben Torres* COL 6–2 6–4 6–0 | *Giovanni Lapentti* ECU d. *Ruben Torres* COL 7–6(2) 6–1 | *Luis Morejon* ECU d. *Pablo Gonzalez* COL 6–7(7) 6–4 7–6(4)

Peru defeated Bahamas 4–1, Lima PER; Clay (O)

Americo Venero PER d. *Mark Knowles* BAH 6–4 6–4 3–6 3–1 ret. | *Luis Horna* PER d. *Mark Merklein* BAH 6–4 6–4 6–4 | *Mark Knowles/Mark Merklein* BAH d. *Luis Horna/Americo Venero* PER 6–3 6–2 4–2 ret. | *Luis Horna* PER d. *Mark Knowles* BAH 6–2 2–6 6–4 3–1 ret. | *Ivan Miranda* PER d. *Dentry Mortimer* BAH 6–1 6–0

Second Round • 7–9 April

Chile defeated Argentina 5–0, Santiago CHI; Hard (I)

Marcelo Rios CHI d. *Hernan Gumy* ARG 6–4 6–3 4–6 6–1 | *Mariano Zabaleta* ARG led *Nicolas Massu* CHI 7–5 2–6 7–6(1) 3–1–match suspended. Argentina subsequently withdrew and the tie was awarded to Chile

Ecuador defeated Peru 3–2, Lima PER; Clay (O)

Luis Horna PER d. *Giovanni Lapentti* ECU 2–6 6–3 6–4 6–1 | *Nicolas Lapentti* ECU d. *Ivan Miranda* PER 6–1 6–2 6–2 | *Luis Horna/Americo Venero* PER d. *Andres Gomez/Nicolas Lapentti* ECU 6–2 6–2 2–6 6–7(3) 7–5 | *Nicolas Lapentti* ECU d. *Luis Horna* PER 4–6 6–2 7–5 6–7(2) 6–3 | *Luis Morejon* ECU d. *Americo Venero* PER 6–3 3–6 6–2 6–1 | Ecuador qualified for World Group Qualifying Round

Second Round/Playoff • 21–23 July

Canada defeated Argentina 4–1, Montreal, Hard (O)

Daniel Nestor CAN d. *Juan Ignacio Chela* ARG 6–3 7–6(3) 6–3 | *Agustin Calleri* ARG d. *Sebastien Lareau* CAN 6–3 6–2 6–3 | *Sebastien Lareau/Daniel Nestor* CAN d. *Martin Garcia/Martin Rodriguez* ARG 6–2 6–1 6–3 | *Sebastien Lareau* CAN d. *Juan Ignacio Chela* ARG 6–3 6–4 4–6 2–6 6–4 | *Daniel Nestor* CAN d. *Agustin Calleri* ARG 6–3 6–2

Bahamas defeated Colombia 3–2, Nassau BAH; Hard (O)

Carlos Drada COL d. *Mark Knowles* BAH 6–7(5) 5–7 2–2 (30-30) ret. | *Mark Merklein* BAH d. *Eduardo Rincon* COL 6–4 6–4 6–4 | *Mark Knowles/Mark Merklein* BAH d. *Carlos Drada/Pablo Gonzalez* COL 6–1 6–4 6–2 | *Eduardo Rincon* COL d. *Roger Smith* BAH 7–6(1) 4–6 1–6 6–1 6–1 | *Mark Merklein* BAH d. *Pablo Gonzalez* COL 7–5 7–6(4) 6–3

3rd Round/Playoff • 6–8 October

Argentina defeated Colombia 4–1, Bogota COL; Clay (O)

Franco Squillari ARG d. *Eduardo Rincon* COL 6–4 6–2 6–2 | *Mariano Puerta* ARG d. *Pablo Gonzalez* COL 6–0 6–2 3–6 6–0 | *Martin Garcia/Mariano Puerta* ARG d. *Michael Quintero/Pablo Gonzalez* COL 6–4 7–5 6–2 | *Agustin Calleri* ARG d. *Pablo Gonzalez* COL 6–3 6–1 | *Michael Quintero* COL d. *Martin Garcia* ARG 7–5 2–6 6–3 | Colombia relegated to American Zone Group II in 2001

Asia/Oceania Zone, First Round • 28–30 January

Uzbekistan defeated China PR 3–0, Kun Ming CHN; Hard (O)

Vadim Kutsenko UZB d. *Ben-Qiang Zhu* CHN 6–4 6–7(5) 6–3 6–7(2) 6–3 | *Oleg Ogorodov* UZB d. *Yu Zhang* CHN 7–6(5) 6–3 6–4 | *Oleg Ogorodov/Dmitri Tomashevich* UZB d. *Ran Xu/Jing-Zhu Yang* CHN 7–6(1) 7–6(1) 6–3 | Reverse singles not played–bad weather

4–6 February

New Zealand defeated Thailand 4–1, Timaru NZL; Hard (O)

Mark Nielsen NZL d. *Danai Udomchoke* THA 6–1 6–1 6–3 | *Alistair Hunt* NZL d. *Paradorn Srichaphan* THA 7–6(6) 7–6(7) 3–6 6–1 | *James Greenhalgh/Alistair Hunt* NZL d. *Ekkarin Pisuth-Arnonth/Wittaya Samrej* THA 6–1 6–0 6–2 | *Mark Nielsen* NZL d. *Ekkarin Pisuth-Arnonth* THA 6–2 7–5 | *Danai Udomchoke* THA d. *James Shortall* NZL 6–7(4) 7–6(4) 6–1

India defeated Lebanon 3–2, Lucknow IND; Grass (O)

Leander Paes IND d. *Ali Hamadeh* LIB 6–4 7–5 7–6(3) | *Fazalludin Syed* IND d. *Jisham Zaatini* LIB 6–4 3–6 7–5 7–6(3) | *Ali Hamadeh/Jisham Zaatini* LIB d. *Leander Paes/Fazalludin Syed* IND 6–7(2) 7–6(3) 4–6 6–3 6–4 | *Leander Paes* IND d. *Jisham Zaatini* LIB 6–3 6–1 6–4 | *Ali Hamadeh* LIB d. *Fazalludin Syed* IND 2–6 7–5 6–1

Korea defeated Japan 3–2, Kashima JPN; Carpet (I)

Hyung-Taik Lee KOR d. *Yaoki Ishii* JPN 4–6 4–6 6–2 6–1 10–8 | *Gouichi Motomura* JPN d. *Yong-Il Yoon* KOR 6–3 4–6 6–4 2–6 6–3 | *Hyung-Taik*

Lee/Yong-Il Yoon KOR d. *Satoshi Iwabuchi/Thomas Shimada* JPN 7–6(4) 6–4 3–6 6–2 | *Hyung-Taik Lee* KOR d. *Gouichi Motomura* JPN 7–5 6–4 7–5 | *Yaoki Ishii* JPN d. *Hee-Sung Chung* KOR 6–4 6–4

Second Round • 7–9 April

Uzbekistan defeated New Zealand 4–1, Tashkent UZB; Hard (I)
Vadim Kutsenko UZB d. *Mark Nielsen* NZL 7–6(3) 6–3 6–2 | *Oleg Ogorodov* UZB d. *Alistair Hunt* NZL 7–6(2) 6–2 6–7(4) 7–5 | *Oleg Ogorodov/Dmitri Tomashevich* UZB d. *James Greenhalgh/Alistair Hunt* NZL 7–5 7–6(5) 6–4 | *Mark Nielsen* NZL d. *Oleg Ogorodov* UZB 6–2 1–6 7–5 *Dmitri Mazur* UZB d. *James Greenhalgh* NZL 7–6(2) 6–4

India defeated Korea 4–1, New Delhi IND; Grass (O)
Leander Paes IND d. *Yong-Il Yoon* KOR 6–4 6–2 6–3 | *Hyung-Taik Lee* KOR d. *Fazaluddin Syed* IND 6–4 7–5 6–2 | *Leander Paes/Vishal Uppal* IND d. *Hyung-Taik Lee/Yong-Il Yoon* KOR 67(5) 6–4 6–4 7–6(4) | *Leander Paes* IND d. *Hyung-Taik Lee* KOR 6–1 3–6 7–6(3) 6–4 | *Fazaluddin Syed* IND d. *Seung-Hun Lee* KOR 6–0 6–7(2) 6–2 | Uzbekistan and India qualified for World Group Qualifying Round

Second Round/Playoff • 7–9 April

Thailand defeated China PR 4–1, Tian Jin CHN; Hard (I)
Paradorn Srichaphan THA d. *Yu Zhang* CHN 6–3 6–2 6–1 | *Ben-Qiang Zhu* CHN d. *Danai Udomchoke* THA 76(5) 6–2 6–0 | *Paradorn Srichaphan/Danai Udomchoke* THA d. *Si Li/Ran Xu* CHN 62 67(7) 2–6 6–3 6–4 | *Paradorn Srichaphan* THA d. *Ben-Qiang Zhu* CHN 7–5 6–3 6–4 | *Danai Udomchoke* THA d. *Yu Zhang* CHN 6–2 6–4

Japan defeated Lebanon 4–1, Yokohamashi JPN; Carpet (I)
Yaoki Ishii JPN d. *Jicham Zaatini* LIB 6–4 6–3 6–3 | *Gouichi Motomura* JPN d. *Ali Hamadeh* LIB 6–3 6–3 6–1 | *Ali Hamadeh/Jicham Zaatini* LIB d. *Satoshi Iwabuchi/Thomas Shimada* JPN 7–6(6) 6–4 6–4 | *Gouichi Motomura* JPN d. *Jicham Zaatini* LIB 6–1 5–7 6–4 6–4 | *Yaoki Ishii* JPN d. *Ali Hamadeh* LIB 6–2 6–4

3rd Round/Playoff • 6–8 October

China PR defeated Lebanon 3–2, Beirut LIB; Hard (I)
Jicham Zaatini LIB d. *Yu Wang* CHN 2–6 6–3 6–3 7–5 | *Ben-Qiang Zhu* CHN d. *Ali Hamadeh* LIB 4–6 6–4 6–3 6–4 | *Ran Xu/Ben-Qiang Zhu* CHN d. *Ali Hamadeh/Jicham Zaatini* LIB 3–6 7–6(9) 6–4 7–5 | *Ben-Qiang Zhu* CHN d. *Jicham Zaatini* LIB 4–6 6–3 6–4 6–4 | *Ali Hamadeh* LIB d. *Yu Zhang* CHN 7–6(6) 7–5 | Lebanon relegated to Asia/Oceania Zone Group II in 2001

GROUP II

Euro/African Zone, First Round • 28–30 April

Croatia defeated Latvia 5–0, Jurmala LAT; Carpet (I)
Goran Ivanisevic CRO d. *Girts Dzelde* LAT 6–1 6–4 6–4 | *Ivan Ljubicic* CRO d. *Andris Filimonovs* LAT 7–6(0) 7–6(6) 6–4 | *Goran Ivanisevic/Ivan Ljubicic* CRO d. *Girts Dzelde/Andris Filimonovs* LAT 6–4 3–6 6–3 6–2 | *Mario Ancic* CRO d. *Raimonds Sproga* LAT 6–3 6–4 | *Lovro Zovko* CRO d. *Ivo Lagzdins* LAT 6–3 6–4

Ireland defeated Luxembourg 3–2, Mondorf-les-Bains LUX; Clay (O)
Scott Barron IRL d. *Mike Scheidweiler* LUX 6–3 6–4 6–4 | *Gilles Muller* LUX d. *Peter Clarke* IRL 6–4 7–5 7–5 | *Scott Barron/Owen Casey* IRL d. *Johny Goudenbour/Mike Scheidweiler* LUX 6–3 6–3 6–4 | *Peter Clarke* IRL d. *Mike Scheidweiler* LUX 6–4 5–7 3–6 7–5 6–2 | *Gilles Muller* LUX d. *Sean Cooper* IRL 6–2 2–6 6–3

Denmark defeated Turkey 3–2, Tarabya TUR; Hard (O)
Frederik Fetterlein DEN d. *Erhan Oral* TUR 6–3 6–4 6–0 | *Kristian Pless* DEN d. *Efe Ustundag* TUR 6–3 7–6(5) 6–1 | *Mustafa Azkara/Erhan Oral* TUR d. *Kristian Pless/Jonathan Printzlau* DEN 6–4 7–6(4) 6–3 | *Kristian Pless* DEN d. *Erhan Oral* TUR 6–2 6–1 6–4 | *Baris Ergun* TUR d. *Bob Borella* DEN 6–7(5) 6–3 ret.

Cote d'Ivoire defeated Lithuania 3–2, Siauliai LTU; Carpet (I)
Claude N'Goran CIV d. *Aivaras Balzekas* LTU 6–3 6–2 6–2 | *Rolandas Murashka* LTU d. *Valentin Sanon* CIV 7–6(4) 7–5 6–3 | *Ilou Lonfo/Claude N'Goran* CIV d. *Paulius Jurkenas/Rolandas Murashka* LTU 6–2 6–7(5) 6–3 6–4 | *Aivaras Balzekas* LTU d. *Valentin Sanon* CIV 7–5 6–3 6–4 | *Claude N'Goran* CIV d. *Rolandas Murashka* LTU 76(3) 4–6 6–3 6–4

Slovenia defeated Egypt, Cairo EGY, Clay (O)

Karim Maamoun EGY d. *Marko Tkalec* SLO 3–6 7–6(5) 7–6(2) 6–7(5) 6–4 | *Andrej Kracman* SLO d. *Amr Ghoneim* EGY 4–6 7–5 4–6 7–6(6) 8–6 | *Andrej Kracman/Marko Tkalec* SLO d. *Amr Ghoneim/Karim Maamoun* EGY 6–1 6–3 6–1 | *Marko Tkalec* SLO d. *Amr Ghoneim* EGY 6–7(1) 6–0 5–7 6–2 6–4 | *Karim Maamoun* EGY d. *Miha Gregorc* SLO 3–6 6–3 6–4

Poland defeated Estonia 4–1, Bytom POL; Clay (O)
Rene Busch EST d. *Bartlomiej Dabrowski* POL 7–6(5) 2–6 6–4 6–0 | *Krystian Pfeiffer* POL d. *Mait Kunnap* EST 6–3 6–7(6) 6–2 6–7(5) 6–1 | *Marcin Matkowski/Radoslav Nijaki* POL d. *Mait Kunnap/Alti Vakhal* EST 6–2 7–6(8) 6–7(5) 6–4 | *Bartlomiej Dabrowski* POL d. *Alti Vahkal* EST 6–2 6–3 6–0 | *Marcin Matkowski* POL d. *Rene Busch* EST 6–2 3–6 6–1

Greece defeated Bulgaria 3–2, Sofia BUL; Clay (O)
Ivailo Traykov BUL d. *Solon Peppas* GRE 6–1 6–3 7–6(2) | *Orlin Stanoytchev* BUL d. *Vasilis Mazarakis* GRE 6–2 1–6 6–3 6–2 | *Konstantinos Economidis/Tasos Vasiliadis* GRE d. *Ivailo Traykov/Orlin Stanoytchev* BUL 3–6 7–6(1) 6–4 7–6(5) | *Solon Peppas* GRE d. *Orlin Stanoytchev* BUL 6–1 3–6 6–1 6–2 | *Vasilis Mazarakis* GRE d. *Milen Velev* BUL 7–6(5) 6–2 6–0

Norway defeated Israel 3–2, Oslo NOR; Clay (O)
Christian Ruud NOR d. *Eyal Ran* ISR 6–2 6–2 7–5 | *Harel Levy* ISR d. *Jan-Frode Andersen* NOR 7–6(6) 6–3 6–4 | *Christian Ruud/Helge Koll* NOR d. *Noam Behr/Andy Ram* ISR 6–4 1–6 6–2 7–6(5) | *Harel Levy* ISR d. *Christian Ruud* NOR 4–6 7–6(5) 6–2 6–7(4) 6–1 | *Jan-Frode Andersen* NOR d. *Andy Ram* ISR 6–4 6–1 7–5

Second Round • 14–16 July

Croatia defeated Ireland 5–0, Dublin IRL; Artificial Grass (O)
Goran Ivanisevic CRO d. *Owen Casey* IRL 7–5 4–6 6–2 6–2 | *Mario Ancic* CRO d. *Scott Barron* IRL 4–6 6–1 6–4 6–4 | *Goran Ivanisevic/Ivo Karlovic* CRO d. *Scott Barron/Owen Casey* IRL 67(5) 6–2 6–1 6–1 | *Ivo Karlovic* CRO d. *Conor Niland* IRL 4–6 6–3 6–4 | *Lovro Zovko* CRO d. *Owen Casey* IRL 1–6 6–4 7–6(3)

21–23 July

Cote dílvoire defeated Denmark 3–2, Rungsted Kyst DEN; Clay (O)
Claude NíGoran CIV d. *Kristian Pless* DEN 7–6(4) 6–2 6–3 | *Valentin Sanon* CIV d. *Frederik Fetterlein* DEN 6–0 4–6 6–2 6–3 | *Illou Lonfo/Claude NíGoran* CIV d. *Frederik Fetterlein/Kristian Pless* DEN 6–4 1–6 6–2 6–3 | *Patrik Langvardt* DEN d. *Valentin Sanon* CIV 7–5 6–0 | *Bob Borella* DEN d. *Illou Lonfo* CIV 6–2 6–3

Slovenia defeated Poland 3–2, Szczecin POL; Clay (O)
Marko Tkalec SLO d. *Bartlomiej Dabrowski* POL 6–1 7–6(3) 7–6(1) | *Krystian Pfeiffer* POL d. *Andrej Kracman* SLO 6–3 6–2 4–6 3–6 6–3 | *Krzysztof Kwinta/Marcin Matkowski* POL d. *Andrej Kracman/Marko Tkalec* SLO 6–4 6–4 7–6(3) | *Marko Tkalec* SLO d. *Krystian Pfeiffer* POL 7–5 6–4 6–4 | *Andrej Kracman* SLO d. *Bartlomiej Dabrowski* POL 6–2 4–6 7–6(5) 6–2

Greece defeated Norway 4–1, Athens GRE; Clay (O)
Solon Peppas GRE d. *Helge Koll* NOR 6–4 6–4 6–3 | *Jan-Frode Andersen* NOR d. *Vassilis Mazarakis* GRE 6–3 6–4 6–7(5) 2–6 6–4 | *Konstantinos Economidis/Taso Vasiliadis* GRE d. *Stian Boretti/Helge Koll* NOR 6–3 6–1 6–2 | *Solon Peppas* GRE d. *Jan-Frode Andersen* NOR 7–5 6–2 6–2 | *Konstantinos Economidis* GRE d. *Stian Boretti* NOR 6–3 6–0

3rd Round • 6–8 October

Croatia defeated Cote D'Ivoire 5–0, Rijeka CRO; Hard (I)
Goran Ivanisevic CRO d. *Claude N'Goran* CIV 6–4 6–4 6–3 | *Ivan Ljubicic* CRO d. *Valentin Sanon* CIV 6–3 7–6(6) 6–3 | *Goran Ivanisevic/Ivo Karlovic* CRO d. *Ilou Lonfo/Claude N'Goran* CIV 7–6(6) 6–4 6–7(5) 4–6 6–0 | *Mario Ancic* CRO d. *Valentin Sanon* CIV 7–5 6–2 | *Ivo Karlovic* CRO d. *Claude N'Goran* CIV 6–4 6–1

Slovenia defeated Greece 4–1, Athens GRE; Clay (O)
Marko Tkalec SLO d. *Nicolas Rovas* GRE 6–2 6–3 2–6 6–1 | *Solon Peppas* GRE d. *Andrej Kracman* SLO 6–4 6–4 6–4 | *Andrej Kracman/Borut Urh* SLO d. *Konstantinos Economidis/Taso Vasiliadis* GRE 2–6 6–4 75 6–3 | *Marko Tkalec* SLO d. *Solon Peppas* GRE 7–5 6–2 7–6(2) | *Andrej Kracman* SLO d. *Konstantinos Economidis* GRE 6–3 2–6 6–3 | Croatia and Slovenia promoted to Euro/African Zone Group I in 2001

Second Round/Playoff • 14–16 July

Luxembourg defeated Latvia 4–1, Mondorf-les-Bains LUX; Clay (O)
Gilles Muller LUX d. *Girts Dzelde* LAT 6–2 6–0 6–2 | *Pascal Schaul* LUX d. *Andris Filimonovs* LAT 6–4 2–6 7–6(6) 7–6(3) | *Johny Goudenbour/Gilles Muller* LUX d. *Girts Dzelde/Andris Filimonovs* LAT 6–3 63 67(9) 75 | *Raimonds Sproga* LAT d. *Sacha Thoma* LUX 6–2 7–5 | *Pascal Schaul* LUX d. *Ivo Lagzdins*

LAT 6–3 5–7 6–2

Turkey defeated Lithuania 4–1, Izmir TUR; Hard (O)
Rolandas Muraska LTU d. *Efe Ustundag* TUR 7–5 6–0 6–4 | *Mustafa Azkara* TUR d. *Aivaras Balzekas* LTU 4–6 6–7(5) 6–4 6–2 9–7 | *Mustafa Azkara/Erhan Oral* TUR d. *Paulius Jurkenas/Rolandas Muraska* LTU 6–4 6–3 6–1 | *Efe Ustundag* TUR d. *Aivaras Balzekas* LTU 4–6 6–1 6–3 6–4 | *Baris Ergun* TUR d. *Rolandas Muraska* LTU 3–6 6–4 7–6(7)

Estonia defeated Egypt 5–0, Tallinn EST; Wood (I)
Gert Vilms EST d. *Karim Maamoun* EGY 7–6(3) 6–2 6–4 | *Andrei Luzgin* EST d. *Hisham Hemeda* EGY 6–7(7) 7–5 6–2 6–2 | *Mait Kunnap/Alti Vahkal* EST d. *Hisham Hemeda/Marwan Zewar* EGY 7–6(3) 6–2 6–4 | *Andrei Luzgin* EST d. *Karim Maamoun* EGY 6–4 7–6(5) | *Mait Kunnap* EST d. *Marwan Zewar* EGY 3–6 6–4 6–3

Israel defeated Bulgaria 3–2, Sofia BUL; Clay (O)
Harel Levy ISR d. *Milen Velev* BUL 6–1 6–3 6–2 | *Ivailo Traykov* BUL d. *Lior Mor* ISR 7–6(4) 4–6 6–4 6–4 | *Todor Enev/Radoslav Lukaev* BUL d. *Jonathan Erlich/Harel Levy* ISR 64 75 76(5) | *Harel Levy* ISR d. *Ivailo Traykov* BUL 6–7(5) 7–6(8) 7–6(3) 7–6(6) | *Lior Mor* ISR d. *Todor Enev* BUL 6–3 6–3 7–5 | Latvia, Lithuania, Egypt and Bulgaria relegated to Euro/African Zone Group III in 2001

American Zone, First Round • 4–6 February
Venezuela defeated Uruguay 5–0, Caracas VEN; Hard (O)
Maurice Ruah VEN d. *Federico Dondo* URU 7–6(5) 6–4 6–3 | *Jimy Szymanski* VEN d. *Alejandro Olivera* URU 7–6(3) 6–4 6–4 | *Jose De Armas/Maurice Ruah* VEN d. *Federico Dondo/Alejandro Olivera* URU 1–6 6–4 4–6 6–3 6–4 | *Jose De Armas* VEN d. *Alberto Brause* URU 6–4 7–6(5) | *Johny Romero* VEN d. *Alejandro Olivera* URU 6–3 6–0

Paraguay defeated El Salvador 5–0, San Salvador ESA; Clay (O)
Francisco Rodriguez PAR d. *Manuel Tejada* ESA 7–6(1) 7–5 6–3 | *Paulo Carvallo* PAR d. *Yari Bernardo* ESA 5–7 7–6(6) 6–3 6–1 | *Paulo Carvallo/Francisco Rodriguez* PAR d. *Yari Bernardo/Miguel Merz* ESA 6–4 6–4 7–6(6) | *Paulo Carvallo* PAR d. *Manuel Tejada* ESA 7–6(4) 6–3 | *Francisco Rodriguez* PAR d. *Jose Baires* ESA 6–3 6–1

Guatemala defeated Cuba 4–1, Guatemala City GUA; Hard (O)
Jacobo Chavez GUA d. *Lazaro Navarro* CUB 7–5 4–6 4–6 6–3 6–4 | *Luis Perez-Chete* GUA d. *Sandor Martinez* CUB 6–4 6–2 6–2 | *Daniel Chavez/Luis Perez-Chete* GUA d. *Sandor Martinez/Lazaro Navarro* CUB 7–6(4) 6–4 6–3 | *Luis Perez-Chete* GUA d. *Kerlin Leon* CUB 3–6 6–3 6–3 | *Sandor Martinez* CUB d. *Jorge Tejada* GUA 6–3 7–5

Mexico defeated Costa Rica 4–1, San Jose CRC; Hard (O)
Rafael Brenes CRC d. *Marco Osorio* MEX 2–6 6–7(2) 7–6(8) 6–1 6–4 | *Alejandro Hernandez* MEX d. *Luis-Diego Nunez* CRC 6–0 6–2 6–0 | *Oscar Ortiz/David Roditi* MEX d. *Alejandro Madrigal/Felipe Montenegro* CRC 6–1 6–2 6–0 | *Alejandro Hernandez* MEX d. *Rafael Brenes* CRC 6–3 6–2 7–6(5) | *Marco Osorio* MEX d. *Luis-Diego Nunez* CRC 6–0 6–1

Second Round • 7–9 April
Venezuela defeated Paraguay 5–0, Caracas VEN; Hard (O)
Jimy Szymanski VEN d. *Emilio Baez-Britez* PAR 6–2 6–1 6–2 | *Jose De Armas* VEN d. *Paulo Carvallo* PAR 7–6(5) 7–5 6–3 | *Jose De Armas/Jimy Szymanski* VEN d. *Emilio Baez-Britez/Paulo Carvallo* PAR 6–2 6–4 6–2 | *Johny Romero* VEN d. *Paulo Carvallo* PAR 6–3 2–6 6–3 | *Oscar Posada* VEN d. *Emilio Baez-Britez* PAR 6–1 6–4

Mexico defeated Guatemala 5–0, Guatemala City GUA; Hard (O)
Alejandro Hernandez MEX d. *Luis Perez-Chete* GUA 6–2 6–3 5–7 6–2 | *Marco Osorio* MEX d. *Jacobo Chavez* GUA 7–5 6–3 6–4 | *Oscar Ortiz/David Roditi* MEX d. *Daniel Chavez/Jacobo Chavez* GUA 6–3 7–5 6–2 | *Alejandro Hernandez* MEX d. *Daniel Chavez* GUA 6–3 6–4 | *Marco Osorio* MEX d. *Alexander Vasquez* GUA 6–2 6–3

Final Round • 21–23 July
Mexico defeated Venezuela 5–0, Mexico City MEX; Hard (O)
Alejandro Hernandez MEX d. *Jose De Armas* VEN 6–2 6–1 6–4 | *Mariano Sanchez* MEX d. *Jimmy Szymanski* VEN 7–6(6) 6–1 6–4 | *Alejandro Hernandez/David Roditi* MEX d. *Jose De Armas/Jimmy Szymanski* VEN 7–6(4) 2–6 6–2 7–6(4) | *Alejandro Hernandez* MEX d. *Jimmy Szymanski* VEN 7–6(2) 6–4 | *Mariano Sanchez* MEX d. *Jose De Armas* VEN 6–0 3–6 6–2 | Mexico promoted to American Zone Group I in 2001

Playoff • 7–9 April
Uruguay defeated El Salvador 4–1, Montevideo ESA; Clay (O)
Alberto Brause URU d. *Manuel Tejada* ESA 6–0 6–4 6–0 | *Federico Dondo* URU d. *Yari Bernardo* ESA 6–1 6–4 6–0 | *Miguel Merz/Augusto Sanabria* ESA

d. *Federico Dondo/Alejandro Olivera* URU 7–5 2–6 6–7(5) 6–3 7–5 | *Federico Dondo* URU d. *Manuel Tejada* ESA 6–3 6–2 6–2 | *Marcel Felder* URU d. *Augusto Sanabria* ESA 6–2 6–1

Costa Rica defeated Cuba 3–2, San Rafael CRC; Hard (O)
Lazaro Navarro CUB d. *Rafael Brenes* CRC 6–4 6–4 6–4 | *Juan Antonio Marin* CRC d. *Kerlin Leon-Zamora* CUB 6–2 6–0 6–2 | *Federico Camacho/Juan Antonio Marin* CRC d. *Sandor Martinez/Lazaro Navarro* CUB 7–6(4) 6–4 5–7 5–7 6–3 | *Juan Antonio Marin* CRC d. *Lazaro Navarro* CUB 6–4 4–6 6–1 4–6 6–4 | *Ricardo Chile* CUB d. *Rafael Brenes* CRC 6–4 6–0 | El Salvador and Cuba relegated to American Zone Group III in 2001

Asia/Oceania Zone, First Round • 28–30 January
Pakistan defeated China Hong Kong 3–2, Causeway Bay HKG; Hard (O)
Melvin Tong HKG d. *Asim Shafik* PAK 6–2 6–1 6–4 | *Aisam Qureshi* PAK d. *Wayne Wong* HKG 6–7(7) 6–4 4–6 7–5 6–3 | *Aisam Qureshi/Ahmad Wahla* PAK d. *Melvin Tong/Andrew Town* HKG 7–6(6) 4–6 4–6 6–3 6–4 | *Aisam Qureshi* PAK d. *Melvin Tong* HKG 4–6 6–1 6–4 6–2 | *Wayne Wong* HKG d. *Aqeel Khan* PAK 7–5 6–4

4–6 February
Chinese Taipei defeated Kazakhstan 4–1, Almaty KAZ; Hard (I)
Wei-Jen Cheng TPE d. *Pavel Baranov* KAZ 6–4 6–4 4–6 7–5 | *Bing-Chao Lin* TPE d. *Alexei Kedriouk* KAZ 6–7(5) 6–1 6–4 5–7 6–4 | *Chih-Jung Chen/Bing-Chao Lin* TPE d. *Pavel Baranov/Alexei Kedriouk* KAZ 6–4 6–1 4–6 6–3 | *Alexei Kedriouk* KAZ d. *Wei-Jen Cheng* TPE 7–5 6–2 | *Chia-Yen Tsai* TPE d. *Dias Doskaraev* KAZ 4–6 7–5 6–1

Malaysia defeated Iran 3–2, Kuala Lumpur MAS; Hard (I)
Ramin Raziani IRI d. *Hazuan Hizan* MAS 6–2 6–2 6–1 | *Selvam Veerasingam* MAS d. *Akbar Taheri* IRI 5–7 7–6(4) 6–4 4–6 7–5 | *Ramin Raziani/Akbar Taheri* IRI d. *Vasuthevan Ortchuan/Selvam Veerasingam* MAS 6–3 1–6 6–3 6–4 | *Selvam Veerasingam* MAS d. *Ramin Raziani* IRI 6–4 6–4 6–4 | *Hazuan Hizan* MAS d. *Akbar Taheri* IRI 6–4 6–2 6–3

Indonesia defeated Philippines 4–1, Manila PHI; Hard (O)
Suwandi Suwandi INA d. *Johnny Arcilla* PHI 6–4 6–2 6–2 | *Febi Widhiyanto* INA d. *Adelo Abadia* PHI 6–4 6–2 6–3 | *Edy Kusdaryanto/Hendri-Susilo Pramono* INA d. *Adelo Abadia/Johnny Arcilla* PHI 6–4 6–2 6–7(4) 5–7 6–1 | *Johnny Arcilla* PHI d. *Febi Widhiyanto* INA 6–0 3–6 6–4 | *Suwandi Suwandi* INA d. *Roland Ruel* PHI 6–4 6–1

Second Round • 7–9 April
Chinese Taipei defeated Pakistan 3–2, Tai-Chung TPE; Clay (O)
Bing-Chao Lin TPE d. *Asim Shafik* PAK 6–1 6–0 6–0 | *Aisam-ul-Haq Qureshi* PAK d. *Chia-Yen Tsai* TPE 6–4 7–6(2) 7–5 | *Aisam-ul-Haq Qureshi/Ahmed Wahla* PAK d. *Wei-Jen Cheng/Bing-Chao Lin* TPE 6–4 6–4 6–4 | *Bing-Chao Lin* TPE d. *Aisam-ul-Haq Qureshi* PAK 2–6 6–2 6–3 6–3 | *Chia-Yen Tsai* TPE d. *Aqeel Khan* PAK 6–0 6–3 6–3

Indonesia defeated Malaysia 5–0, Kuala Lumpur MAS; Hard (I)
Suwandi Suwandi INA d. *Ortchun Vasuthevan* MAS 6–2 6–2 6–3 | *Febi Widhiyanto* INA d. *Selvam Veerasingam* MAS 6–3 6–3 6–2 | *Sulistyo Wibowo/Bonit Wiryawan* INA d. *Mohammed-Nazreen Fuzi/Selvam Veerasingam* MAS 6–4 6–2 6–1 | *Febi Widhiyanto* INA d. *Mohammed Nazreen Fuzi* MAS 6–0 6–1 | *Suwandi Suwandi* INA d. *Adam Jaya* MAS 6–1 6–1

Final • 6–8 October
Indonesia defeated Chinese Taipei 4–1, Jakarta INA; Hard (O)
Suwandi Suwandi INA d. *Wei-Jen Cheng* TPE 6–4 6–2 6–2 | *Hendri-Susilo Pramono* INA d. *Chia-Yen Tsai* TPE 6–4 7–6(3) 6–3 | *Sulistyo Wibowo/Bonit Wiryawan* INA d. *Wei-Ju Chen/Wei-Jen Cheng* TPE 6–3 6–4 6–4 | *Suwandi Suwandi* INA d. *Chia-Yen Tsai* TPE 6–3 5–7 6–1 | *Wei-Jen Cheng* TPE d. *Hendri-Susilo Pramono* INA 6–4 6–2 | Indonesia promoted to Asia/Oceania Zone Group I for 2001

Playoff • 17–19 March
Iran defeated Philippines 3–2, Manila PHI; Clay (I)
Johnny Arcilla PHI d. *Mohammad Reza Tavakoli* IRI 6–3 6–4 6–3 | *Ramin Raziani* IRI d. *Adelo Abadia* PHI 7–6(7) 7–6(4) 6–2 | *Johnny Arcilla/Michael Misa* PHI d. *Ramin Raziani/Akbar Taheri* IRI 6–3 3–6 6–3 7–6(5) | *Ramin Raziani* IRI d. *Johnny Arcilla* PHI 6–4 6–4 7–6(5) | *Anosha Shagholi* IRI d. *Rolando Ruel* PHI 4–6 6–3 6–3 6–1

7–9 April
China Hong Kong defeated Kazakhstan 3–2, Hong Kong HKG; Hard (O)
Melvin Tong HKG d. *Pavel Baranov* KAZ 3–6 6–3 6–4 7–5 | *Alexey Kedryuk* KAZ d. *Wayne Wong* HKG 6–2 6–2 6–2 | *Chris Numbers/Melvin Tong* HKG d. *Pavel Baranov/Alexey Kedryuk* KAZ 7–5 7–6(6) 6–1 | *Alexey Kedryuk* KAZ d.

Melvin Tong HKG 6–3 3–6 6–1 3–6 6–2 | *Wayne Wong* HKG d. *Pavel Baranov* KAZ 6–4 4–6 7–6(5) 6–2 | Philippines and Kazakhstan relegated to Asia/Oceania Zone Group III in 2001

GROUP III

Date 24–28 May | Venue Tunis, Tunisia | Surface Clay (O) | Group A Bosnia/Herzegovina, Georgia, Malta, Togo | Group B Botswana, Monaco, Tunisia, Yugoslavia

Group A

Bosnia/Herzegovina defeated Togo 2–1

Haris Basalic BIH d. *Jean-Kome Loglo* TOG 6–3 6–1 | *Merid Zahirovic* BIH d. *Kossi-Essaram Loglo* TOG 6–0 6–0 | *Jean-Kome Loglo/Kossi-Essaram Loglo* TOG d. *Ismar Gorcic/Merid Zahirovic* BIH 6–1 7–5

Georgia defeated Malta 3–0

Konstantin Burchuladze GEO d. *Marco Cappello* MLT 6–1 6–1 | *Irakli Ushangishvili* GEO d. *Mark Schembri* MLT 6–4 2–6 6–4 | *Otari Enukidze/Irakli Ushangishvili* GEO d. *Luke Bonello/Matthew Debono* MLT 2–6 6–4 6–3

Bosnia/Herzegovina defeated Georgia 3–0

Haris Basalic BHA d. *Konstantin Burchuladze* GEO 6–0 6–2 | *Merid Zahirovic* BHA d. *Irakli Ushangishvili* GEO 6–1 6–2 | *Ismar Gorcic/Goran Houdek* BHA d. *Konstantin Burchuladze/Otari Enukidze* GEO 6–7(2) 6–1 7–5

Togo defeated Malta 3–0

Komlavi Loglo TOG d. *Matthew Debono* MLT 6–2 6–1 | *Kossi-Essaram Loglo* TOG d. *Mark Schembri* MLT 6–3 6–3 | *Komlavi Loglo/Kossi-Essaram Loglo* TOG d. *Luke Bonello/Matthew Debono* MLT 6–2 6–1

Bosnia/Herzegovina v Malta

Haris Basalic BIH d. *Luke Bonello* MLT 6–4 6–2 | Second singles and doubles matches cancelled due to rain–final position in Group not affected

Georgia defeated Togo 2–1

Jean-Kome Loglo TOG d. *Otari Enukidze* GEO 6–2 6–2 | *Irakli Ushangishvili* GEO d. *Kossi-Essaram Loglo* TOG 6–2 6–7(4) 6–4 | *David Katcharava/Irakli Ushangishvili* GEO d. *Kamlavi Loglo/Kossi-Essaram Loglo* TOG 7–5 6–2.

Group B

Botswana defeated Tunisia 2–1

Michael Judd BOT d. *Chekib Jemai* TUN 4–6 6–0 11–9 | *Fares Zaier* TUN d. *Petrus Molefe* BOT 5–7 6–4 6–2 | *Michael Judd/Petrus Molefe* BOT d. *Chakib Jemai/Youssef Miled* TUN 6–2 5–7 6–3

Yugoslavia defeated Monaco 3–0

Nenad Zimonjic YUG d. *Emmanuel Heussner* MON 6–4 3–6 6–0 | *Dusan Vemic* YUG d. *Christophe Bosio* MON 6–3 6–3 | *Relja Dulic-Fiser/Janko Tipsarevic* YUG d. *Christophe Bosio/Emmanuel Heussner* MON 6–3 7–6(3)

Yugoslavia defeated Botswana 3–0

Relja Dulic-Fiser YUG d. *Lesedi Bewlay* BOT 6–0 6–1 | *Nenad Zimonjic* YUG d. *Petrus Molefe* BOT 6–3 6–0 | *Janko Tipsarevic/Dusan Vemic* YUG d. *Michael Judd/Petrus Molefe* BOT 6–4 6–0

Monaco defeated Tunisia 3–0

Emmanuel Heussner MON d. *Malek Jaziri* TUN 6–1 6–2 | *Christophe Bosio* MON d. *Youssef Miled* TUN 6–1 6–1 | *Christophe Bosio/Axel Mellet* MON d. *Chekib Jemai/Fares Zaier* TUN 4–6 6–3 6–4

Monaco defeated Botswana 2–0

Emmanuel Heussner MON d. *Michael Judd* BOT 7–5 6–4 | *Christophe Bosio* MON d. *Petrus Molefe* BOT 6–4 6–2 | Doubles match cancelled due to rain–final position in Group not affected

Yugoslavia defeated Tunisia 2–0

Janko Tipsarevic YUG d. *Chekib Jemai* TUN 6–3 6–2 *Nenad Zimonjic* YUG d. *Youssef Miled* TUN 6–4 6–0 | Doubles match cancelled due to rain–final position in Group not affected

Yugoslavia defeated Georgia 3–0

Nenad Zimonjic YUG d. *Konstantin Burchuladze* GEO 6–1 6–3 | *Dusan Vemic* YUG d. *Irakli Ushangishvili* GEO 6–3 6–1 | *Relja Dulic-Fiser/Janko Tipsarevic* YUG d. *Konstantin Burchuladze/Otari Enukidze* GEO 6–2 6–3

Monaco defeated Bosnia/Herzegovina 2–1

Emmanuel Heussner MON d. *Haris Basalic* BIH 3–6 6–0 8–6 | *Merid Zahirovic* NIH d. *Christophe Bosio* MON 3–6 6–1 6–3 | *Christophe Bosio/Emmanuel Heussner* MON d. *Haris Basalic/Goran Houdek* BIH 6–3 7–6(7)

Yugoslavia defeated Monaco 3–0

Nenad Zimonjic YUG d. *Emmanuel Heussner* MON 6–1 6–0 | *Dusan Vemic* YUG d. *Christophe Bosio* MON 6–3 6–1 | *Relja Dulic-Fiser/Janko Tipsarevic* YUG d. *Christophe Boggetti/Emmanuel Heussner* MON 7–5 6–2

Georgia defeated Bosnia/Herzegovina 2–1

Konstantin Burchuladze GEO d. *Ismar Gorcic* BIH 6–0 6–2 | *Irakli Ushangishvili* GEO d. *Goran Houdek* BIH 7–5 6–0 | *Ismar Gorcic/Goran Houdek* BIH d. *Konstantin Burchuladze/Otari Enukidze* GEO 6–4 6–2

Botswana defeated Malta 3–0

Michael Judd BOT d. *Matthew Debono* MLT 5–7 6–2 7–5 | *Petrus Molefe* BOT d. *Mark Schembri* MLT 7–6(7) 6–2 | *Lesedi Bewlay/Karabo Makgale* BOT d. *Luke Bonello/Mark Schembri* MLT 6–1 0–6 6–3

Togo defeated Tunisia 2–1

Chekib Jemai TUN d. *Komi Adeyo* TOG 6–3 6–3 | *Komlavi Loglo* TOG d. *Youssef Miled* TUN 6–2 1–6 6–0 | *Jean-Kome Loglo/Kossi-Essaram Loglo* TOG d. *Chekib Jamai/Fares Zaier* TUN 6–3 6–1

Togo defeated Botswana 3–0

Jean-Kome Loglo TOG d. *Michael Judd* BOT 7–6(2) 6–2 | *Kossi-Essaram Loglo* TOG d. *Petrus Molefe* BOT 7–6(4) 6–0 | *Komi Adeyo/Komlavi Loglo* TOG d. *Michael Judd/Karabo Makgale* BOT 6–3 6–4

Tunisia defeated Malta 2–1

Luke Bonello MLT d. *Malek Jaziri* TUN 4–6 6–3 6–2 | *Chekib Jemai* TUN d. *Matthew Debono* MLT 7–5 6–0 | *Chekib Jamai/Fares Zaier* TUN d. *Luke Bonello/Matthew Debono* MLT 6–3 7–6(3)

Final Positions: 1. Yugoslavia, 2. Monaco, 3. Georgia, 4. Bosnia/Herzegovina, 5. Togo, 6. Botswana, 7. Tunisia, 8. Malta | Yugoslavia and Monaco promoted to Euro/African Zone Group II in 2001 | Tunisia and Malta relegated to Euro/African Zone Group IV in 2001.

Date 24–28 May | Venue Antananarivo, Madagascar | Surface Clay (O) | Group A Benin, Iceland, Moldova, Senegal | Group B Armenia, FYR of Macedonia, Madagascar, Nigeria

Group A

Moldova defeated Senegal 3–0

Yuri Gorban MDA d. *Djadji Ka* SEN 6–2 6–3 | *Evgueni Plougarev* MDA d. *Daouda Senga Ndiaye* SEN 6–3 7–6(3) | *Yuri Gorban/Evgueni Plougarev* MDA d. *Djadi Ka/Daouda Senga Ndiaye* SEN 7–5 7–5

Iceland defeated Benin 3–0

Raj Bonifacius ISL d. *Arnaud Segodo* BEN 6–3 6–0 | *Arnar Sigurdsson* ISL d. *Alphonse Gandonou* BEN 6–3 6–1 | *David Halldorsson/Arnar Sigurdsson* ISL d. *Jean-Marie Da Silva/Alphonse Gandonou* BEN 6–4 6–4

Moldova defeated Iceland 3–0

Yuri Gorban MDA d. *David Halldorsson* ISL 6–0 6–0 | *Evgueni Plougarev* MDA d. *Arnar Sigurdsson* ISL 6–3 7–5 | *Andrei Gorban/Victor Ribas* MDA d. *David Halldorsson/Arnar Sigurdsson* ISL 6–4 6–3

Senegal defeated Benin 2–1

Wael Zeidan SEN d. *Souron Gandonou* BEN 6–3 6–3 | *Daouda Senga Ndiaye* SEN d. *Alphonse Gandonou* BEN 6–3 6–2 | *Alphonse Gandonou/Arnaud Segodo* BEN d. *Djadji Ka/Wael Zeidan* SEN 6–3 6–4

Moldova defeated Benin 3–0

Yuri Gorban MDA d. *Arnaud Segodo* BEN 6–2 6–3; | *Evgueni Plougarev* MDA d. *Sourou Gandonou* BEN 6–2 6–2 | *Andrei Gorban/Victor Ribas* MDA d. *Alphonse Gandonou/Jean-Marie Da Silva* BEN 6–4 4–6 6–2

Iceland defeated Senegal 2–1

Raj Bonifacius ISL d. *Wael Zeidan* SEN 6–4 7–6(3) | *Arnar Sigurdsson* ISL d. *Daouda Senga Ndiaye* SEN 6–4 6–0 | *Daouda Senga Ndiaye/Wael Zeidan* SEN d. *David Halldorsson/Jon Axel Jonsson* ISL 6–2 7–6(4)

Group B

FYR of Macedonia defeated Nigeria 3–0
Predrag Rusevski MKD d. *Ganiyu Adelekan* NGR 4–6 6–1 6–4 | *Zoran Sevcenko* MKD d. *Sule Ladipo* NGR 5–7 7–5 6–2 | *Kristijan Mitrovski/ Predrag Rusevski* MKD d. *Ganiyu Adelekan/Sule Ladipo* NGR 6–3 6–2

Armenia defeated Madagascar 3–0
Tsolak Gevorgyan ARM d. *Alexis Rafidison* MAD 6–4 3–6 6–4 | *Sargis Sargsian* ARM d. *Lalaina Ratsimbazafy* MAD 7–6(3) 6–0 | *Tsolak Gevorgyan/Sargis Sargsian* ARM d. *Harivony Andrianafetra/Jean Marc Randriamanalina* MAD 6–4 6–1

Armenia defeated FYR of Macedonia 2–1
Zoran Sevcenko MKD d. *Tsolak Gevorgyan* ARM 6–3 6–3 | *Sargis Sargsian* ARM d. *Kristijan Mitrovski* MKD 2–6 6–3 6–2 | *Tsolak Gevorgyan/Sargis Sargsian* ARM d. *Predrag Rusevski/Zoran Sevcenko* MKD 6–1 6–1

Madagascar defeated Nigeria 2–1
Alexis Rafidison MAD d. *Ganiyu Adelekan* NGR 6–2 6–1 | *Sule Ladipo* NGR d. *Jean Marc Randriamanalina* MAD 7–6(6) 6–3 | *Harivony Andrianafetra/Alexis Rafidison* MAD d. *Ganiyu Adelekan/Sule Ladipo* NGR 7–6(7) 6–3

Armenia defeated Nigeria 2–1
Ganiyu Adelekan NGR d. *Harutiun Sofian* ARM 7–5 7–5 | *Sargis Sargsian* ARM d. *Sule Ladipo* NGR 6–3 6–3 | *Tsolak Gevorgyan/Sargis Sargsian* ARM d. *Ganiyu Adelekan/Sule Ladipo* NGR 6–4 6–4

FYR of Macedonia defeated Madagascar 2–1
Zoran Sevcenko MKD d. *Alexis Rafidison* MAD 6–4 6–3 | *Jean Marc Randriamanalina* MAD d. *Kristijan Mitrovski* MKD 2–6 6–3 6–4 | *Predrag Rusevski/Zoran Sevcenko* MKD d. *Harivony Andrianafetra/Alexis Rafidison* MAD 6–3 1–6 6–1

Playoff for 1st–4th Positions

Moldova defeated FYR of Macedonia 2–1
Yuri Gorban MDA d. *Predrag Rusevski* MKD 7–5 3–6 6–4 | *Evgueni Plougarev* MDA d. *Zoran Sevcenko* MKD 7–5 1–6 7–5 | *Kristijan Mitrovski/Predrag Rusevski* MKD d. *Andrei Gorban/Victor Ribas* MDA 6–3 6–1

Armenia defeated Iceland 3–0
Tsolak Gevorgyan ARM d. *Raj Bonifacius* ISL 7–6(5) 7–5 | *Sargis Sargsian* ARM d. *Arnar Sigurdsson* ISL 6–3 6–2 | *Haik Hakobian/Harutiun Sofian* ARM d. *David Halldorsson/Arnar Sigurdsson* ISL 6–7(5) 6–3 6–4

Playoff for 1st/2nd Position

Moldova defeated Armenia 2–1
Andrei Gorban MDA d. *Harutiun Sofian* ARM 4–6 7–6(5) 7–5 | *Victor Ribas* MDA d. *Tsolak Gevorgyan* ARM 6–4 6–4 | *Haik Hakobian/Harutiun Sofian* ARM d. *Andrei Gorban/Victor Ribas* MDA 5–7 7–5 6–4

Playoff for 3rd/4th Position

Iceland defeated FYR of Macedonia 2–1
Zoran Sevcenko MKD d. *Raj Bonifacius* ISL 6–2 6–2 | *Arnar Sigurdsson* ISL d. *Kristijan Mitrovski* MKD 6–3 6–3 | *Raj Bonifacius/Arnar Sigurdsson* ISL d. *Kristijan Mitrovski/Predrag Rusevski* MKD 6–3 6–4

Playoff for 5th–8th Positions

Nigeria defeated Senegal 2–1
Ganiyu Adelekan NGR d. *Wael Ziedan* SEN 4–6 6–1 6–3 | *Sule Ladipo* NGR d. *Daouda Senga Ndiaye* SEN 6–2 7–5 | Nigeria forfeited doubles

Madagascar defeated Benin 3–0
Alexis Rafidison MAD d. *Arnaud Segodo* BEN 6–1 6–2 | *Lalaina Ratsimbazafy* MAD d. *Alphonse Gandonou* BEN 6–3 6–2 | *Jean Marc Randriamanalina/ Lalaina Ratsimbazafy* MAD d. *Alphonse Gandonou/Arnaud Segodo* BEN 4–6 6–3 6–4

Playoff for 5th/6th Position

Nigeria defeated Madagascar 2–1
Alexis Rafidison MKD d. *Ganiyu Adelekan* NGR 6–1 0–1 ret. | *Sule Ladipo* NGR d. *Lalaina Ratsimbazafy* MKD 6–1 6–3 | *Bulus Hussaini/Sule Ladipo* NGR d. *Harivony Andrianafetra/Jean Marc Randriamanalina* MAD 6–2 6–4

Playoff for 7th/8th Position

Benin defeated Senegal 3–0
Arnaud Segodo BEN d. *Wael Zeidan* SEN 6–4 6–7(3) 6–3 | *Alphonse Gandonou* BEN d. *Daouda Senga Ndiaye* SEN 6–5 def | *Alphonse Gandonou/Arnaud Segodo* BEN d. *Youssou Berthe/Djadji Ka* SEN 6–3 6–1

Final Positions 1. Moldova, 2. Armenia, 3. Iceland, 4. FYR of Macedonia, 5. Nigeria, 6. Madagascar, 7. Benin, 8. Senegal | Moldova and Armenia promoted to Euro/African Zone Group II in 2001 | Benin and Senegal relegated to Euro/African Zone Group IV in 2001

American Zone

Date 24–28 March | **Venue** Kingston, Jamaica | **Surface** Clay O) | **Group A** Haiti, Jamaica, Panama, Puerto Rico | **Group B** Bolivia, Dominican Republic, Netherlands Antilles, Trinidad & Tobago

Group A

Jamaica defeated Panama 3–0
Ryan Russell JAM d. *Juan Pablo Herrera* PAN 7–6(6) 6–1 | *Jermaine Smith* JAM d. *Chad Valdez* PAN 6–3 7–6(4) | *Nakia Gordon/Scott Willinsky* JAM d. *Braen Aneiros/Arnulfo Courney* PAN 6–3 7–5

Puerto Rico defeated Haiti 2–1
Juan Carlos Fernandez PUR d. *Joel Allen* HAI 6–1 6–4 | *Gabriel Montilla* PUR d. *Jerry Joseph* HAI 6–2 6–4 | *Joel Allen/Jerry Joseph* HAI d. *Stephen Diaz/Luis Haddock* PUR 2–6 6–3 6–4

Puerto Rico defeated Jamaica 2–1
Ryan Russell JAM d. *Juan-Carlos Fernandez* PUR 6–3 6–4 | *Gabriel Montilla* PUR d. *Jermaine Smith* JAM 4–6 6–3 6–2 | *Stephen Diaz/ Gabriel Montilla* PUR d. *Nakia Gordon/Ryan Russell* JAM 7–6(4) 2–6 6–1

Panama defeated Haiti 2–1
Juan Pablo Herrera PAN d. *Joel Allen* HAI 5–7 7–5 6–3 | *Chad Valdez* PAN d. *Jerry Joseph* HAI 6–3 7–5 | *Joel Allen/Jerry Joseph* HAI d. *Braen Aneiros/Arnulfo Courney* PAN 3–6 6–1 6–3

Jamaica defeated Haiti 3–0
Ryan Russell JAM d. *Carl-Henry Barthold* HAI 6–1 6–0 | *Jermaine Smith* JAM d. *Jerry Joseph* HAI 6–7(4) 6–2 6–2 | *Nakia Gordon/Scott Willinsky* JAM d. *Jean-Claude Augustin/Carl-Henry Barthold* HAI 6–2 6–2

Puerto Rico defeated Panama 3–0
Luis Haddock PUR d. *Juan Pablo Herrera* PAN 4–6 7–6(4) 6–2 | *Gabriel Montilla* PUR d. *Chad Valdez* PAN 6–0 6–2 | *Stephen Diaz/Juan-Carlos Fernandez* PUR d. *Braen Aneiros/Arnulfo Courney* PAN 5–7 6–1 9–7

Group B

Trinidad & Tobago defeated Dominican Republic 2–1
Simon Evelyn TRI d. *Genaro De Leon* DOM 6–2 2–6 6–4 | *Rodrigo Vallejo* DOM d. *Shane Stone* TRI 1–6 7–6(3) 8–6 | *Shane Stone/Troy Stone* TRI d. *Sixto Camacho/Rodrigo Vallejo* DOM 6–4 6–7(4) 6–2

Netherlands Antilles defeated Bolivia 3–0
Elmar Gerth AHO d. *Daniel Chavarria* BOL 6–2 6–4 | *Jean-Julien Rojer* AHO d. *Jose Antelo* BOL 6–3 6–3 | *Raoul Behr/Kevin Jonckheer* AHO d. *Rodrigo Navarro/Rodrigo Villarroel* BOL 6–3 ret.

Dominican Republic defeated Bolivia 2–1
Daniel Chavarria BOL d. *Victor Estrella* DOM 6–4 6–4 | *Genaro de Leon* DOM d. *Jose Antelo* BOL 6–0 6–3 | *Sixto Camacho/Rodrigo Vallejo* DOM d. *Daniel Chavarria/Rodrigo Villarroel* BOL 6–4 3–6 6–1

Netherlands Antilles defeated Trinidad & Tobago 3–0
Elmar Gerth AHO d. *Simon Evelyn* TRI 6–2 6–3 | *Jean-Julien Rojer* AHO d. *Shane Stone* TRI 6–3 6–3 | *Raoul Behr/Kevin Jonckheer* AHO d. *Shane Stone/Troy Stone* TRI 6–2 2–6 6–2

Bolivia defeated Trinidad & Tobago 3–0
Rodrigo Navarro BOL d. *Randy Hakim* TRI 6–3 6–3 | *Jose Antelo* BOL d. *Simon Evelyn* TRI 4–6 6–2 6–2 | *Jose Antelo/Daniel Chavarria* BOL d. *Simon Evelyn/Troy Stone* TRI 4–6 6–1 6–4

Netherlands Antilles defeated Dominican Republic 2–1
Elmar Gerth AHO d. *Genaro De Leon* DOM 6–2 6–7(1) 6–4 | *Jean-Julien Rojer* AHO d. *Rodrigo Vallejo* DOM 6–1 7–6(3) | *Sixto Camacho/Rodrigo Vallejo* DOM d. *Raoul Behr/Kevin Jonckheer* AHO 7–5 3–6 6–3

Playoff for 1st–4th Positions

Dominican Republic defeated Puerto Rico 2–1
Genaro De Leon DOM d. *Juan-Carlos Fernandez* PUR 6–4 6–4 | *Rodrigo Vallejo* DOM d. *Stephen Diaz* PUR 6–4 6–7(4) 6–3 | *Juan-Carlos Fernandez/ Luis Haddock* PUR d. *Sixto Camacho/Victor Estrella* DOM 6–2 6–4

Netherlands Antilles defeated Jamaica 2–1
Ryan Russell JAM d. *Elmar Gerth* AHO 4–6 6–2 6–4 | *Jean-Julien Rojer* AHO d. *Jermaine Smith* JAM 7–6(4) 6–4 | *Elmar Gerth/Jean-Julien Rojer* AHO d. *Ryan Russell/Jermaine Smith* JAM 6–2 6–1

Playoff for 1st/2nd Position

Netherlands Antilles defeated Dominican Republic 2–1
Elmar Gerth AHO d. *Genaro De Leon* DOM 3–6 6–4 6–3 | *Jean-Julien Rojer* AHO d. *Rodrigo Vallejo* DOM 6–3 6–2 | *Sixto Camacho/Victor Estrella* DOM d. *Raoul Behr/Kevin Jonckheer* AHO 6–2 6–4

Playoff for 3rd/4th Position
Puerto Rico defeated Jamaica 2–1
Ryan Russell JAM d. *Luis Haddock* PUR 3–6 6–4 6–2 | *Juan-Carlos Fernandez* PUR d. *Jermaine Smith* JAM 61 5–7 6–4 | *Juan-Carlos Fernandez/Luis Haddock* PUR d. *Nakia Gordon/Ryan Russell* PUR 2–6 6–1 6–2

Playoff for 5th–8th Positions
Trinidad & Tobago defeated Panama 2–1
Juan Pablo Herrera PAN d. *Simon Evelyn* TRI 6–3 6–4 | *Shane Stone* TRI d. *Chad Valdez* PAN 6–4 6–3 | *Simon Evelyn/Troy Stone* TRI d. *Braen Aneiros/Juan Pablo Herrera* PAN 6–3 6–4

Bolivia defeated Haiti 2–1
Joel Allen HAI d. *Rodrigo Villarroel* BOL 6–1 6–3 | *Rodrigo Navarro* BOL d. *Jerry Joseph* HAI 6–2 6–1 | *Jose Antelo/Rodrigo Navarro* BOL d. *Joel Allen/Jerry Joseph* HAI 3–6 6–0 6–3

Playoff for 5th/6th Position
Bolivia defeated Trinidad & Tobago 3–0
Rodrigo Navarro BOL d. *Randy Hakim* TRI 6–0 6–3 | *Jose Antelo* BOL d. *Simon Evelyn* TRI 7–6(5) 6–1 | *Rodrigo Navarro/Rodrigo Villarroel* BOL d. *Randy Hakim/Troy Stone* TRI 6–4 6–1

Playoff for 7th/8th Position
Panama defeated Haiti 3–0
Juan Pablo Herrera PAN d. *Jean-Claude Augustin* HAI 6–1 3–6 6–3 | *Arnulfo Courney* PAN d. *Carl-Henry Barthold* HAI 6–3 6–3 | *Arnulfo Courney/Chad Valdez* PAN d. *Joel Allen/Jerry Joseph* HAI 6–2 6–4

Final Positions: 1. Netherlands Antilles, 2. Dominican Republic, 3. Puerto Rico, 4. Jamaica, 5. Bolivia, 6. Trinidad & Tobago, 7. Panama, 8. Haiti | Netherlands Antilles and Dominican Republic promoted to American Zone Group II in 2001 | Panama and Haiti relegated to American Zone Group IV in 2001

Asia/Oceania Zone

Date 7–13 February | Venue Colombo, Sri Lanka | Surface Clay (O) | Group A Bangladesh, Kuwait, Pacific Oceania, Qatar | Group B Singapore, Sri Lanka, Syria, Tajikistan

Group A
Kuwait defeated Bangladesh 3–0
Hamed Al-Solaiteen KUW d. *Moin-ud-din Walliullah* BAN 3–6 6–4 6–0 | *Mohammed Al-Ghareeb* KUW d. *Nadeem-Kamran Khan* BAN 6–2 6–2 | *Mohammed-Rashid Al-Foudari /Adel Al-Shatti* KUW d. *Dilip Passia/Moin-ud-din Walliullah* BAN 5–7 6–2 7–5

Qatar defeated Pacific Oceania 3–0
Nasser-Ghanim Al-Khulaifi QAT d. *Bret.t Baudinet* POC 6–4 7–5 | *Sultan-Khalfan Al-Alawi* QAT d. *Lency Tenai* POC 6–3 7–5 | *Sultan-Khalfan Al-Alawi/Nasser-Ghanim Al-Khulaifi* QAT d. *Cyril Jacobe/Jerome Rovo* POC 6–4 7–6(5)

Bangladesh defeated Pacific Oceania 2–1
Dilip Passia BAN d. *Jerome Rovo* POC 7–6(5) 3–6 6–1 | *Nadeen-Kamran Khan* BAN d. *Lency Tenai* POC 6–4 4–6 6–3 | *Bret.t Baudinet/Cyril Jacobe* POC d. *Dilip Passia/Moin-ud-din Walliullah* BAN 6–0 6–1

Qatar defeated Kuwait 3–0
Nasser-Ghanim Al-Khulaifi QAT d. *Hamed Al-Solaiteen* KUW 6–2 6–4 | *Sultan-Khalfan Al-Alawi* QAT d. *Mohammed Al-Ghareeb* KUW 6–4 3–1 ret. | *Sultan-Khalfan Al-Alawi/Mohammed-Ali Al-Saoud* QAT d. *Mohammed-Rashid Al-Foudari/Hammed Al-Sloulaiteen* KUW 7–6(6) 6–7(4) 6–3

Kuwait defeated Pacific Oceania 2–1
Bret.t Baudinet POC d. *Hamed Al-Solaiteen* KUW 1–6 6–4 6–3 | *Mohammed Al-Ghareeb* KUW d. *Lency Tenai* POC 3–6 6–1 6–4 | *Mohammed-Rashid Al-Foudari/Mohammed Al-Ghareeb* KUW d. *Cyril Jacobe/Jerome Rovo* POC 6–7(3) 6–1 6–3

Bangladesh defeated Qatar 2–1
Moin-ud-Walliullah BAN d. *Nasser-Ghanim Al-Khulaifi* QAT 6–4 3–0 ret. | *Sultan-Khalfan Al-Alawi* QAT d. *Dilip Passia* BAN 6–2 6–1 | *Dilip Passia/Moin-ud-din Walliullah* BAN d. *Sultan-Khalfan Al-Alawi/Mohammed-Ali Al-Saoud* QAT 6–1 7–6(5)

Group B
Syria defeated Tajikistan 2–1
Samir Saad El Din SYR d. *Sergei Makashin* TJK 7–6(2) 6–1 | *Rabi Bou-Hassoun* SYR d. *Mansur Yakhyaev* TJK 3–6 7–6(5) 6–2 | *Sergei Makashin/Mansur Yakhyaev* TJK d. *Rabi Bou-Hassoun/Lais Salim* SYR 6–1 6–2

Sri Lanka defeated Singapore 3–0
Jayendra Wijeyesekera SRI d. *Tung-Yi Kho* SIN 6–2 6–2 | *Rohan De Silva* SRI d. *Sian Yang* SIN 6–3 6–4 | *Asiri Iddamalgoda/Jayendra Wijeyesekera* SRI d. *Jensen Hiu/Tung-Yi Kho* SIN 6–3 6–2

Sri Lanka defeated Tajikistan 2–1
Jayendra Wijeyesekera SRI d. *Sergei Makashin* TJK 6–1 6–0 | *Mansur Yakhyaev* TJK d. *Rohan De Silva* SRI 6–3 6–3 | *Rohan De Silva/Jayendra Wijeyesekera* SRI d. *Sergei Makashin/Mansur Yakhyaev* TJK 3–6 6–3 6–2

Syria defeated Singapore 2–1
Lais Salim SYR d. *Jensen Hiu* SIN 6–0 0–6 6–3 | *Rabi Bou-Hassoun* SYR d. *Sian Yang* SIN 6–0 6–0 | *Jensen Hiu/Sian Yang* SIN d. *Abdul-Rahim Salim/Lais Salim* SYR 7–5 6–3

Sri Lanka defeated Syria 2–1
Jayendra Wijeyesekera SRI d. *Samir Saad El Din* SYR 6–3 6–4 | *Rabi Bou-Hassoun* SYR d. *Rohan de Silva* SRI 6–3 6–4 | *Rohan De Silva/Jayendra Wijeyesekera* SRI d. *Abdul-Rahim Salim/Lais Salim* SYR 6–2 7–5

Tajikistan defeated Singapore 2–1
Sergei Makashin TJK d. *Jensen Hiu* SIN 7–5 6–1 | *Mansur Yakhyaev* TJK d. *Sian Yang* SIN 6–2 6–3 | *Kyoung Sik Seol/Tung-Yi Kho* SIN d. *Sergei Makashin/Sergei Sedov* TJK 6–1 6–1

Playoff for 1st–4th Positions
Syria defeated Qatar 2–0
Samir Saad El Din SYR d. *Nasser-Ghanim Al-Khulaifi* QAT 7–6(2) 6–3 | *Rabi Bou-Hassoun* SYR d. *Sultan-Khalfan Al-Alawi* QAT 6–3 6–1 | *Rabi Bou-Hassoun/Lais Salim* SYR v *Sultan-Khalfan Al-Alawi/Mohammed-Ali Al-Saoud* QAT–not played

Kuwait defeated Sri Lanka 2–1
Jayendra Wijeyesekera SRI d. *Hamed Al-Solaiteen* KUW 6–3 6–7(2) 6–2 | *Mohammed Al-Ghareeb* KUW d. *Rohan De Silva* SRI 6–1 6–2 | *Mohammed-Rashid Al-Foudari/Mohammed Al-Ghareeb* KUW d. *Rohan De Silva/Jayendra Wijeyesekera* SRI 6–3 7–6(4)

Playoff for 1st/2nd Position
Syria defeated Kuwait 2–1
Lais Salim SYR d. *Hamed Al-Solaiteen* KUW 6–2 6–1 | *Rabi Bou-Hassoun* SYR d. *Mohammed Al-Ghareeb* KUW 6–4 7–6(4) | *Mohammed-Rashid Al-Foudari/Adel Al-Shatti* KUW d. *Abdul-Rahim Salim/Lais Salim* SYR 7–6(4) 2–6 6–4

Playoff for 3rd/4th Position
Sri Lanka defeated Qatar 2–1
Nasser-Ghanim Al-Khulaifi QAT d. *Sanjeev Paramanathan* SRI 7–6(8) 6–1 | *Asiri Iddamalgoda* SRI d. *Sultan-Khalfan Al-Alawi* QAT 6–4 6–2 | *Asiri Iddamalgoda/Rohan De Silva* SRI d. *Sultan-Khalfan Al-Alawi/Nasser-Ghanim Al-Khulaifi* QAT 6–4 7–5

Playoff for 5th–8th Positions
Singapore defeated Bangladesh 2–1
Moin-ud-Walliullah BAN d. *Tung-Yi Kho* SIN 6–3 6–4 | *Sian Yang* SIN d. *Nadeem-Kamran Khan* BAN 6–4 7–6(2) | *Jensen Hiu/Kyoung Sik Seol* SIN d. *Dilip Passia/Moin-ud-din Walliullah* BAN 6–2 7–6(4)

Tajikistan defeated Pacific Oceania 2–0
Sergei Makashin TJK d. *Bret.t Baudinet* POC 7–5 6–4 | *Mansur Yakhyaev* TJK d. *Lency Tenai* POC 6–3 6–0 | *Sergei Makashin/Mansur Yakhyaev* TJK v *Bret.t Baudinet/Lency Tenai* POC–not played

Playoff for 5th/6th Position
Tajikistan defeated Singapore 2–1
Sergei Makashin TJK d. *Tung-Yi Kho* SIN 3–6 4–1 ret. | *Mansur Yakhyaev* TJK d. *Sian Yang* SIN 6–4 6–2 | *Jensen Hiu/Sian Yang* SIN d. *Sergei Makashin/Sergei Sedov* TJK 6–3 6–4

Playoff for 7th/8th Position
Bangladesh defeated Pacific Oceania 2–1
Cyril Jacobe POC d. *Dilip Passia* BAN 6–1 6–2 | *Nadeem-Kamran Khan* BAN d. *Jerome Rovo* POC 6–4 6–2 | *Dilip Passia/Abu-Hena-Tasawar Collins* BAN d. *Bret.t Baudinet/Lency Tenai* BAN 3–6 6–4 9–7

Final Positions: 1. Syria, 2. Kuwait, 3. Sri Lanka, 4. Qatar, 5. Tajikistan, 6. Singapore, 7. Bangladesh, 8. Pacific Oceania | Syria and Kuwait promoted to Asia/Oceania Group II for 2001 | Bangladesh and Pacific Oceania relegated to Asia/Oceania Group IV for 2001

GROUP IV

Euro/African Zone—Venue 1

Date 14-20 February | Venue Accra, Ghana | Surface Hard (O) | Group A Algeria, Andorra, Liechtenstein, Sudan | Group B Azerbaijan, Cameroon, Ghana, Mauritius

Group A

Algeria defeated Liechtenstein 3–0
Noureddine Mahmoudi ALG d. *Andreas Schweiger* LIE 6–1 6–0 | *Abdelhak Hameurlaine* ALG d. *Alexander Risch* LIE 6–3 6–0 | *Sid Ali Akkal/Abdel-Wahid Henni* ALG d. *Kenny Banzer/Wolfgang Strub* LIE 6–0 6–3

Andorra defeated Sudan 3–0
Jean-Baptiste Poux-Gautier AND d. *Mandour Abdalla* SUD 6–0 6–1 | Joan *Jimenez-Guerra* AND d. *Nour Gaafar* SUD 6–0 6–1 | Joan *Jimenez-Guerra/Jean-Baptiste Poux-Gautier* AND d. *Nour Gaafar/Nour Wail* SUD 6–0 6–1

Algeria defeated Sudan 3–0
Noureddine Mahmoudi ALG d. *Mandour Abdalla* SUD 6–2 6–2 | *Abdelhak Hameurlaine* ALG d. *Nour Gaafar* SUD 6–1 6–0 | *Sid Ali Akkal/Abdel-Wahid Henni* ALG d. *Nour Gaafar/Nour Wail* SUD 7–6(2) 6–0

Andorra defeated Liechtenstein 3–0
Jean-Baptiste Poux-Gautier AND d. *Andreas Schweiger* LIE 6–0 6–0 | *Joan Jimenez-Guerra* AND d. *Alexander Risch* LIE 6–0 6–0 | *Joan Jimenez-Gautier/Kenneth Tuilier-Curco* AND d. *Kenny Banzer/Wolfgang Strub* LIE 6–1 6–0

Liechtenstein defeated Sudan 2–1
Andreas Schweiger LIE d. *Mandour Abdalla* SUD 4–6 6–3 7–5 | *Alexander Risch* LIE d. *Nour Gaafar* SUD 6–2 6–3 | *Nour Gaafar/Nour Wail* SUD d. *Kenny Banzer/Wolfgang Strub* LIE 6–1 6–3

Algeria defeated Andorra 2–1
Noureddine Mahmoudi ALG d. *Kenneth Tuilier-Curco* AND 2–6 7–5 6–3 | *Abdelhak Hameurlaine* ALG d. *Joan Jimenez-Guerra* AND 1–6 6–2 6–3 | *Kenneth Tuilier-Curco/Jean-Baptiste Poux-Gautier* AND d. *Sid Ali Akkal/Abdel-Wahid Henni* ALG 6–1 6–1

Group B

Ghana defeated Azerbaijan 3–0
Frank Ofori GHA d. *Nidjat Ramazanov* AZE 6–1 6–1 | *Gunther Darkey* GHA d. *Emin Agaev* AZE 7–6(1) 6–4 | *Courage Anyidoho/Frank Ofori* GHA d. *Talat Rahimov/Farid Shirinov* AZE 6–1 6–1

Mauritius defeated Cameroon 3–0
Jean-Marcel Bourgault Du Coudray MRI d. *Pierre Otolo-Metomo* CMR 6–1 6–4 | *Kamil Patel* MRI d. *Lionel Kemajou* CMR 6–3 6–3 | *Jean-Marcel Bourgault Du Coudray/ Kamil Patel* MRI d. *Luc Ondobo/Pierre Otolo-Metomo* CMR 6–2 6–1

Ghana defeated Mauritius 2–1
Frank Ofori GHA d. *Jean-Marcel Bourgault Du Coudray* MRI 6–4 6–4 | *Gunther Darkey* GHA d. *Kamil Patel* MRI 4–6 7–6(3) 6–2 | *Jean-Marcel Bourgault Du Coudray/Kamil Patel* MRI d. *Courage Anyidoho/Thomas Debrah* GHA 6–2 7–6(6)

Cameroon defeated Azerbaijan 3–0
Pierre Otolo-Metomo CMR d. *Nidjat Ramazanov* AZE 6–1 6–2 | *Lionel Kemajou* CMR d. *Emin Agaev* AZE 6–4 6–1 | *Alifa Adoum/Lionel Kemajou* CMR d. *Talat Rahimov/Farid Shirinov* AZE 6–0 6–1

Ghana defeated Cameroon 3–0
Frank Ofori GHA d. *Pierre Otolo-Metomo* CMR 7–5 7–6(3) | *Gunther Darkey* GHA d. *Lionel Kemajou* CMR 7–6(2) 7–5 | *Gunther Darkey/Frank Ofori* GHA d. *Alifa Adoum/Pierre Otolo-Metomo* CMR 6–2 6–4

Mauritius defeated Azerbaijan 2–1
Jean-Marcel Bourgault Du Coudray MRI d. *Nidjat Ramazanov* AZE 6–2 6–0 | *Emin Agaev* AZE d. *Kamil Patel* MRI 6–7(8) 7–5 6–4 | *Jean-Marcel Bourgault Du Coudray/Jonathan Vencathachellum* MRI d. *Emin Agaev/Nidjat Ramazanov* AZE 6–3 6–3

Playoff for 1st–4th Positions

Mauritius defeated Algeria 2–1
Jean-Marcel Bourgault Du Coudray MRI d. *Noureddine Mahmoudi* ALG 6–4 6–1 | *Abdelhak Hameurlaine* ALG d. *Kamil Patel* MRI 6–7(3) 6–3 6–1 | *Jean-Marcel Bourgault Du Coudray/Kamil Patel* MRI d. *Abdelhak Hameurlaine/Noureddine Mahmoudi* ALG 6–3 6–1

Ghana defeated Andorra 3–0
Frank Ofori GHA d. *Jean-Baptiste Poux-Gautier* AND 7–6(3) 6–3 | *Gunther Darkey* GHA d. *Joan Jimenez-Guerra* AND 6–2 6–4 | *Courage Anyidoho/Thomas Debrah* GHA d. *Kenneth Tuilier-Curco/Jean-Baptiste Poux-Gautier* AND 6–3 6–3

Playoff for 1st/2nd Position

Ghana defeated Mauritius 3–0
Thomas Debrah GHA d. *Jonathan Vencathachellum* MRI 6–3 6–1 | *Courage Anyidoho* GHA d. *Jean-Marcel Bourgault Du Coudray* MRI 4–6 7–6(9) 6–3 | *Courage Anyidoho/Gunther Darkey* GHA d. *Jonathan Vencathachellum/Kenny Wong Kee Chuan* MRI 6–0 6–2

Playoff for 3rd/4th Position

Andorra defeated Algeria 2–1
Kenneth Tuilier-Curco AND d. *Sid Ali Akkal* ALG 3–6 6–2 6–1 | *Noureddine Mahmoudi* ALG d. *Jean-Baptiste Poux-Gautier* AND 4–6 7–6(3) 6–4 | *Joan Jimenez-Guerra/Kenneth Tuilier-Curco* AND d. *Abdelhak Hameurlaine/Abdel-Wahid Henni* ALG 6–4 6–1

Playoff for 5th–8th Positions

Azerbaijan defeated Liechtenstein 2–1
Nidjat Ramazanov AZE d. *Andreas Schweiger* LIE 6–1 2–6 6–1 | *Emin Agaev* AZE d. *Alexander Risch* LIE 6–1 4–6 6–1 | *Kenny Banzer/Andreas Schweiger* LIE d. *Talat Rahimov/Farid Shirinov* AZE 6–4 6–3

Cameroon Defeated Sudan 3–0
Alifa Adoum CMR d. *Nour Wail* SUD 6–4 6–3 | *Luc Ondobo* CMR d. *Nour Gaafar* SUD 6–3 0–6 10–8 | *Alifa Adoum/Luc Ondobo* CMR d. *Nour Gaafar/Nour Wail* SUD 6–4 6–4

Playoff for 5th/6th Position

Cameroon Defeated Azerbaijan 2–1
Pierre Otolo-Metomo CMR d. *Nidjat Ramazanov* AZE 7–6(2) 6–1 | *Emin Agaev* AZE d. *Lionel Kemajou* CMR 6–4 6–3 | *Alifa Adoum/Pierre Otolo-Metomo* CMR d. *Nidjat Ramazanov/Farid Shirinov* AJE 6–3 6–2

Playoff for 7th/8th Position

Liechtenstein defeated Sudan 3–0
Andreas Schweiger LIE d. *Nour Wail* SUD 1–6 6–1 13–11 | *Alexander Risch* LIE d. *Nour Gaafar* SUD 6–0 6–0 | *Kenny Banzer/Alex Risch* LIE d. *Nour Gaafar/Abdella Jeha* SUD 7–6(5) 7–6(1)

Final Positions: 1. Ghana, 2. Mauritius, 3. Andorra, 4. Algeria, 5. Cameroon, 6. Azerbaijan, 7. Liechtenstein, 8. Sudan | Ghana and Mauritius promoted to Euro/African Zone Group III in 2001

Euro/African Zone—Venue 2

Date 19–23 January | Venue Kampala, Uganda | Surface Clay (O) | Group A Ethiopia, Namibia, San Marino, Zambia | Group B Cyprus, Djibouti, Kenya, Lesotho, Uganda

Group A

Zambia defeated San Marino 2–1
Sidney Bwalya ZAM d. *William Forcellini* SMR 6–3 6–0 | *Domenico Vicini* SMR d. *Lighton Ndefwayi* ZAM 7–5 6–3 | Sidney Bwalya/Lighton Ndefwayi ZAM d. *Gabriel Francini/Domenico Vicini* SMR 6–1 6–2

Zambia defeated Ethiopia 2–1
Sidney Bwalya ZAM d. *Yohannes Setegne* ETH 6–2 6–1 | *Samuel Woldegebriel* ETH d. *Lighton Ndefwayi* ZAM 7–5 6–3 | *Sidney Bwalya/Lighton Ndefwayi* ZAM d. *Asfaw Mikaile/Yohannes Setegne* ETH 6–3 6–2

Namibia defeated San Marino 2–1
Jean-Pierre Huish NAM d. *William Forcellini* SMR 6–3 6–2 | *Domenico Vicini* SMR d. *Johan Theron* NAM 6–1 6–1 | *Henrico Du Plessis/Johan Theron* NAM d. *William Forcellini/Domenico Vicini* SMR 6–3 6–3

Namibia defeated Ethiopia 3–0
Jean-Pierre Huish NAM d. *Yohannes Setegne* ETH 6–4 6–1 | *Johan Theron* NAM d. *Samuel Woldegebriel* ETH 6–3 7–5 | *Henrico Du Plessis/Kevin Wentzel* NAM d. *Asfaw Mikaile/Samuel Woldegebriel* ETH 7–5 6–2

Namibia defeated Zambia 2–1
Sidney Bwalya ZAM d. *Jean-Pierre Huish* NAM 6–2 3–6 6–4 | *Johan Theron* NAM d. *Lighton Ndefwayi* ZAM 6–4 6–3 | *Henrico Du Plessis/Johan Theron* NAM d. *Sidney Bwalya/Lighton Ndefwayi* ZAM 6–4 6–4

San Marino defeated Ethiopia 2–1
Yohannes Setegne ETH d. *William Forcellini* SMR 6–3 6–1 | *Domenico Vicini* SMR d. *Samuel Woldegebriel* ETH 6–3 6–3 | *Andrea Della Balda/Domenico Vicini* SMR d. *Asfaw Mikaile/Samuel Woldegebriel* ETH 7–5 3–6 6–3

Final Positions: 1. Namibia, 2. Zambia, 3. San Marino, 4. Ethiopia

Group B

Kenya defeated Uganda 3–0

Allan Cooper KEN d. *Robert Buyinza* UGA 6–3 6–1 | *Trevor Kiruki* KEN d. *Bob Ndibwami* UGA 6–4 3–6 6–1 | *Barry Ndinya/Norbert Oduor* KEN d. *Robert Buyinza/Bob Ndibwami* UGA 7–6(6) 7–6(6)

Cyprus defeated Lesotho 3–0

George Kalanov CYP d. *Khotso Khali* LES 6–3 6–1 | *Demetrios Leondis* CYP d. *Ntsane Moeletsi* LES 6–1 6–0 | *Marcos Baghdatis/Demetrios Leondis* CYP d. *Ntsukunyane Letseka/Relebohile Motsepa* LES 6–2 6–0

Kenya defeated Cyprus 2–1

Allan Cooper KEN d. *George Kalanov* CYP 7–5 4–6 7–5 | *Demetrios Leondis* CYP d. *Trevor Kiruki* KEN 6–4 6–4 | *Allan Cooper/Trevor Kiruki* KEN d. *Marcos Baghdatis/Demetrios Leondis* CYP 6–4 6–3

Lesotho defeated Djibouti 3–0

Relebohile Motsepa LES d. *Alla Mousa* DJI 6–1 6–1 | *Ntsane Moeletsi* LES d. *Kadar Mogueh* DJI 6–1 6–1 | *Khotso Khali/Ntsukunyane Letseka* LES d. *Abdou-Rahman Aden/Kadar Mogueh* DJI 6–4 6–0

Kenya defeated Lesotho 3–0

Barry Ndinya KEN d. *Khotso Khali* LES 6–1 6–4 | *Trevor Kiruki* KEN d. *Ntsane Moeletsi* LES 6–2 6–0 | *Barry Ndinya/Norbert Oduor* KEN d. *Ntsukunyane Letseka/Relebohile Motsepa* LES 6–2 6–4

Uganda defeated Djibouti 3–0

Robert Buyinza UGA d. *Alla Mousa* DJI 6–0 ret. | *Bob Ndibwami* UGA d. *Abdou-Rahman Aden* DJI 6–1 6–0 | *Robert Buyinza/Bob Ndibwami* UGA d. *Alla Mousa/Abdou-Rahman Aden* DJI w/o

Uganda defeated Lesotho 2–1

Relebohile Motsepa LES d. *Robert Buyinza* UGA 7–5 6–3 | *Bob Ndibwami* UGA d. *Ntsane Moeletsi* LES 6–4 3–6 6–4 | *Robert Buyinza/Bob Ndibwami* UGA d. *Ntsukunyane Letseka/Relebohile Motsepa* LES 6–1 6–3

Cyprus defeated Djibouti 3–0

Constantinos Talianos CYP d. *Abdou-Rahman Aden* DJI 6–0 ret. | *Marcos Baghdatis* CYP d. *Kadar Mogueh* DJI 6–0 6–0 | *George Kalanov/Constantinos Talianos* CYP d. *Abdou-Rahman Aden/Kader Mogueh* DJI 6–1 6–0

Cyprus defeated Uganda 2–1

Marcos Baghdatis CYP d. *Robert Buyinza* UGA 6–3 6–4 | *George Kalanov* CYP d. *Bob Ndibwami* UGA 6–2 6–4 | *Robert Buyinza/Bob Ndibwami* UGA d. *Marcos Baghdatis/Constantinos Talianos* CYP 7–6(5) 2–6 6–3

Kenya defeated Djibouti 3–0

Barry Ndinya KEN d. *Abdou-Rahman Aden* DJI 6–1 6–2 | *Allan Cooper* KEN d. *Kadar Mogueh* DJI 6–0 1–0 ret. | *Allan Cooper/Barry Ndinya* KEN d. *Adballah Aden/Abdou-Rahman Aden* DJI 6–0 6–1

Final Positions: 1. Kenya, 2. Cyprus, 3. Uganda, 4. Lesotho, 5. Djibouti | Namibia and Kenya promoted to Euro/African Zone III in 2001

American Zone

Date 13-19 March | **Venue** San Pedro Sula, Honduras | **Surface** Hard (O) | **Nations** Antigua & Barbuda, Bermuda, Honduras, OECS, St. Lucia, US Virgin Islands

Honduras defeated OECS 3–0

Calton Alvarez HON d. *Dexter Christian* ECA 6–0 6–1 | *Carlos Caceres* HON d. *Kirtsen Cable* ECA 6–3 6–1 | *Franklin Garcia/Cristian Kawas* HON d. *Hayden Ashton/Kirtsen Cable* ECA 6–1 4–6 6–3

Bermuda defeated St. Lucia 2–1

Jenson Bascome BER d. *McCollin Fontenelle* LCA 7–5 6–3 | *Kane Easter* LCA d. *James Collieson* BER 6–3 6–3 | *Jenson Bascome/Richard Mallory* BER d. *Sirsean Arlain/Kane Easter* LCA 6–4 6–4

Barbados defeated US Virgin Islands 2–1

Lenin Mongerie ISV d. *Duane Williams* BAR 6–1 3–6 9–7 | *Kodi Lewis* BAR d. *Gregory Newton* ISV 7–5 6–3 | *James Betts/Kodi Lewis* BAR d. *Lenin Mongerie/Gregory Newton* ISV 0–6 6–4 7–5

Honduras defeated Bermuda 3–0

Calton Alvarez HON d. *Richard Mallory* BER 7–5 3–1 ret. | *Carlos Caceres* HON d. *James Collieson* BER 6–0 6–4 | *Carlos Caceres/Cristian Kawas* HON d. *Jenson Bascome/Dean Mello* BER 6–2 6–1

US Virgin Islands defeated Antigua & Barbuda 2–1

Carlton Bedminster ANT d. *Lenin Mongerie* ISV 6–3 4–6 6–4 | *Gregory*

Newton ISV d. *Jerry Williams* ANT 6–3 6–2 | *Gregory Newton/John Richards* ISV d. *Carlton Bedminster/Kevin Gardner* ANT 6–1 6–1

Barbados defeated OECS 2–1

Duane Williams BAR d. *Dexter Christian* ECA 7–6(4) 1–6 6–4 | *Kodi Lewis* BAR d. *Kirtsen Cable* ECA 6–1 6–4 | *Hayden Ashton/Kirtsen Cable* ECA d. *James Betts/Michael Date* BAR 6–4 6–2

St. Lucia defeated Antigua/Barbuda 2–1

Carlton Bedminster ANT d. *McCollin Fontenelle* LCA 6–2 6–1 | *Kane Easter* LCA d. *Jerry Williams* ANT 6–4 6–2 | *Sirsean Arlain/Kane Easter* LCA d. *Carlton Bedminster/Kevin Gardener* ANT 7–6(7) 7–5

OECS defeated US Virgin Islands 2–1

Louis Taylor ISV d. *Dexter Christian* ECA 6–4 6–2 | *Kirtsen Cable* ECA d. *Lenin Mongerie* ISV 1–6 6–1 6–3 | *Hayden Ashton/Kirtsen Cable* ECA d. *Gregory Newton/John Richards* ISV 4–6 6–3 7–5

Bermuda defeated Barbados 2–1

Richard Mallory BER d. *Duane Williams* BAR 6–1 6–2 | *James Collieson* BER d. *Kodi Lewis* BAR 6–4 3–6 6–4 | *James Betts/Duane Williams* BAR d. *Jenson Bascome/Dean Mello* BER 7–5 2–6 7–5

Honduras defeated St. Lucia 3–0

Calton Alvarez HON d. *Sirsean Arlain* LCA 6–1 6–1 | *Carlos Caceres* HON d. *Kane Easter* LCA 6–2 7–6(5) | *Carlos Caceres/Cristian Kawas* HON d. *Sirsean Arlain/Jonathan Jean-Baptiste* LCA 6–3 6–2

Antigua & Barbuda defeated OECS 3–0

Kevin Gardener ANT d. *Dexter Christian* ECA 6–4 6–3 | *Carlton Bedminster* ANT d. *Kirtsen Cable* ECA 3–6 7–6(3) 6–2 | *Jerry Williams/Gershum Philip* ANT d. *Hayden Ashton/Damian Hughes* ECA 6–0 1–6 6–3

Bermuda defeated US Virgin Islands 2–1

Louis Taylor ISV d. *Richard Mallory* BER 4–6 6–3 8–6 | *James Collieson* BER d. *Gregory Newton* ISV 4–6 6–2 6–4 | *Dean Mello/Jenson Bascome* BER d. *Gregory Newton/John Richards* ISV 4–6 6–4 6–4

Honduras defeated Antigua & Barbuda 3–0

Calton Alvarez HON d. *Kevin Gardner* ANT 6–1 6–1 | *Carlos Caceres* HON d. *Carlton Bedminster* ANT 6–3 6–0 | *Carlos Caceres/Christian Kawas* HON d. *Gershum Philip/Jerry Williams* ANT 6–2 6–1

Bermuda defeated OECS 3–0

Jenson Bascome BER d. *Damian Hughes* ECA 6–4 6–1 | *James Collieson* BER d. *Kirtsen Cable* ECA 6–2 7–5 | *Jenson Bascome/Dean Mello* BER d. *Hayden Ashton/Damian Hughes* ECA 6–1 ret.

St. Lucia defeated Barbados 2–1

Sirsean Arlain LCA d. *James Betts* BAR 6–4 6–0 | *Kane Easter* LCA d. *Kodi Lewis* BAR 6–2 6–2 | *James Betts/Kodi Lewis* BAR d. *Sirsean Arlain/Jonathan Jean-Baptiste* LCA 6–7(7) 6–2 7–5

Honduras defeated Barbados 3–0

Calton Alvarez HON d. *Duane Williams* BAR 6–1 6–3 | *Carlos Caceres* HON d. *Kodi Lewis* BAR 6–1 3–6 6–1 | *Carlos Caceres/Christian Kawas* HON d. *James Betts/Duane Williams* BAR 6–2 3–6 6–3

Bermuda defeated Antigua & Barbuda 3–0

Richard Mallory BER d. *Gershum Philip* ANT 6–1 6–1 | *James Collieson* BER d. *Carlton Bedminster* ANT 6–1 7–5 | *Jenson Bascome/Dean Mello* BER d. *Kevin Gardner/Jerry Williams* ANT 6–7(2) 7–6(3) 6–3

St. Lucia defeated US Virgin Islands 3–0

Sirsean Arlain LCA d. *Louis Taylor* ISV 6–3 7–6(5) | *Kane Easter* LCA d. *Lenin Mongerie* ISV 6–2 6–1 | *Sirsean Arlain/Jonathan Jean-Baptiste* LCA d. *Lenin Mongerie/Gregory Newton* ISV 7–6(3) 7–6(3)

Honduras defeated US Virgin Islands 3–0

Franklin Garcia HON d. *John Richards* ISV 7–5 6–4 | *Christian Kawas* HON d. *Gregory Newton* ISV 3–6 6–1 6–2 | *Carlos Caceres/Christian Kawas* HON d. *Gregory Newton/John Richards* ISV 6–4 5–7 7–5

Antigua & Barbuda defeated Barbados 3–0

Kevin Gardner ANT d. *Michael Date* BAR 7–6(4) 6–0 | *Carlton Bedminster* ANT d. *Duane Williams* BAR 7–5 6–2 | *Kevin Gardner/Jerry Williams* ANT d. *James Betts/Kodi Lewis* BAR 3–6 7–6(5) 6–2

St. Lucia defeated OECS 3–0

Sirsean Arlain LCA d. *Dexter Christian* ECA 6–2 6–2 | *Kane Easter* LCA d. *Kirtsen Cable* ECA 6–4 6–2 | *Sirsean Arlain/Kane Easter* LCA d. *Kirtsen Cable/Hayden Ashton* ECA 6–4 6–2

Final Positions: 1. Honduras, 2. Bermuda, 3. St. Lucia, 4. Antigua & Barbuda, 5. Barbados, 6. US Virgin Islands, 7. OECS | Honduras and Bermuda promoted to American Zone Group III in 2001

Date 24–30 April | Venue Amman, Jordan | Surface Hard (O) | Nations Bahrain, Brunei, Fiji, Jordan, Oman, Saudi Arabia, United Arab Emirates

Jordan d. Brunei 2–1

Ahmad Al Hadid JOR d. *Billy Wong* BRU 6–0 6–3 | *Abdalla Fada* JOR d. *Ismasufian Ibrahim* BRU 6–4 6–1 | *Hardiyamin Baharuddin/Ismasufian Ibrahim* BRU d. *Ammar Al Maaytah/Ahmad Al Hadid* JOR 6–3 6–3

Bahrain d. United Arab Emirates 2–1

Essam Abdul-Aal BRN d. *Mahmoud Al Balushi* UAE 6–3 6–1 | *Abdul-Rahman Shehab* BRN d. *Omar-Bahrzrouzyan Awadhy* UAE 6–4 7–5 | *Omar-Bahrzrouzyan Awadhy/Mahmoud Al Balushi* UAE d. *Nader Abdul-Aal/Fahad Sarwani* BRN 7–6(6) 6–3

Oman d. Fiji 3–0

Khalid Al Nabhani OMA d. *Hitesh Morriswala* FIJ 6–2 7–5 | *Mudrik Al Rawahi* OMA d. *Sanjeev Tikaram* FIJ 6–4 7–6(7) | *Khalid Al Nabhani/Mudrik Al Rawahi* OMA d. *Mohammed Jannif/Diva Gawander* FIJ 6–0 6–3

Jordan d. United Arab Emirates 2–1

Ahmad Al Hadid JOR d. *Mahmoud Al Balushi* UAE 3–6 4–4 ret. | *Omar-Bahrzrouzyan Awadhy* UAE d. *Abdalla Fada* JOR 6–3 2–6 6–2 | *Ahmad Al Hadid/Abdalla Fada* JOR d. *Omar-Bahrzrouzyan Awadhy/Abdulla Kamber* UAE 7–6(4) 3–6 7–5

Bahrain d. Fiji 3–0

Essam Abdul-Aal BRN d. *Hitesh Morriswala* FIJ 6–2 6–0 | *Abdul-Rahman Shehab* BRN d. *Sanjeev Tikaram* FIJ 6–2 6–0 | *Essal Abdul-Aal/Nader Abdul-Aal* BRN d. *Hitesh Morriswala/Sanjeev Tikaram* FIJ 6–4 6–0

Oman d. Saudi Arabia 2–1

Badar Al Megayel KSA d. *Khalid Al Nabhani* OMA 6–4 6–4 | *Mudrik Al Rawahi* OMA d. *Abdullah Nour* KSA 4–6 6–3 6–4 | *Khalid Al Nabhani* OMA/*Mudrik Al Rawahi* OMA d. *Baqer Abu Khulaif/Badar Al Megayel* KSA 6–3 7–6(3)

Oman d. Jordan 3–0

Khalid Al Nabhani OMA d. *Ammar Al Maaytah* JOR 7–5 6–2 | *Mudrik Al Rawahi* OMA d. *Ahmad Al Hadid* JOR 4–6 6–4 7–5 | *Mudrik Al Rawahi/Khalid Al Nabhani* OMA d. *Abdalla Fada/Tareq Matekri* JOR 6–2 6–2

Fiji d. United Arab Emirates 2–1

Omar-Bahrzrouzyan Awadhy UAE d. *Hitesh Morriswala* FIJ 6–2 6–3 | *Sanjeev Tikaram* FIJ d. *Othman Al Ulama* UAE 6–1 7–5 | *Hitesh Morriswala/Sanjeev Tikaram* FIJ d. *Othman Al Ulama/Omar-Bahrzrouzyan Awadhy* UAE 6–4 6–3

Saudi Arabia d. Brunei 3–0

Badar Al Megayel KSA d. *Billy Wong* BRU 6–0 6–0 | *Abdullah Nour* KSA d. *Ismasufian Ibrahim* BRU 6–1 6–4 | *Badar Al Megayel/Baqer Abu Khulaif* KSA d. *Ismasufian Ibrahim/Hardiyamin Baharuddin* BRU 6–3 6–2

Saudi Arabia d. Jordan 2–1

Badar Al Megayel KSA d. *Ammar Al Maaytah* JOR 6–1 6–1 | *Ahmad Al Hadid* JOR d. *Abdullah Nour* KSA 3–6 6–4 6–4 | *Badar Al Megayal/Baqer Abu Khulaif* KSA d. *Ahmed Al Hadid/Abdallah Fada* JOR 6–0 4–6 6–0

United Arab Emirates d. Brunei 3–0

Abdulla Kamber UAE d. *Sharill Teo* BRU 6–1 6–2 | *Omar-Bahrzrouzyan Awadhy* UAE d. *Ismasufian Ibrahim* BRU 6–2 6–4 | *Omar-Bahrzrouzyan Awadhy/Abdulla Kamber* UAE d. *Ismasufian Ibrahim/Hardiyamin Baharuddin* BRU 6–0 6–3

Bahrain d. Oman 2–1

Essam Abdul-Aal BRN d. *Khalid Al Nabhani* OMA 4–6 6–3 6–1 | *Mudrik Al Rawahi* OMA d. *Abdul-Rahman Shehab* BRN 6–1 6–7(5) 6–3 | *Essam Abdul-Aal/Abdul-Rahman Shehab* BRN d. *Khalid Al Nabhani/Mudrik Al Rawahi* OMA 6–3 4–6 6–2

Bahrain d. Jordan 2–1

Essam Abdul-Aal BRN d. *Tareq Matekri* JOR 6–0 6–0 | *Ahmed Al-Hadid* JOR d. *Abdul-Rahman Shehab* BRN 6–3 6–3 | *Essam Abdul-Aal/Abdul-Rahman Shehab* BRN d. *Ahmed Al-Hadid/Abdallah Fada* JOR 6–1 6–3

Saudi Arabia d. United Arab Emirates 2–1

Badar Al Megayel KSA d. *Asdulla Kamber* UAE 6–0 6–1 | *Omar-Bahrzrouzyan Awadhy* UAE d. *Abdullah Nour* KSA 2–6 6–4 6–1 | *Badar Al Megayel/Omar Al Thagib* KSA d. *Omar-Bahrzrouzyan Awadhy/Asdulla Kamber* UAE 6–2 6–2

Fiji d. Brunei 3–0

Hitesh Morriswala FIJ d. *Billy Wong* BRU 6–1 6–1 | *Sanjeev Tikaram* FIJ d. *Ismafusian Ibrahim* BRU 6–1 6–3 | *Mohammed Jannif/Hitesh Morriswala* FIJ d. *Sharill Teo/Billy Wong* BRU 6–2 6–3

Bahrain d. Brunei 3–0

Fahad Sarwani BRN d. *Sharrill Fred Teo* BRU 6–1 6–0 | *Essam Abdul-Aal* BRN d. *Billy Wong* BRU 6–0 6–0 | *Nader Abdul-Aal/Abdul-Rahman Shehab* BRN d. *Sharill Teo/Billy Wong* BRU 6–0 6–0

Saudi Arabia d. Fiji 3–0

Badar Al Megayel KSA d. *Mohammed Jannif* FIJ 6–1 6–1 | *Abdullah Nour* KSA d. *Sanjeev Tikaram* FIJ 6–4 4–6 6–4 | *Badar Al Megayel/Omar Al Thagib* KSA d. *Mohammed Jannif/Hitesh Morriswala* FIJ 6–4 7–6(3)

United Arab Emirates d. Oman 2–1

Omar-Bahrzrouzyan Awadhy UAE d. *Khalid Al Nabhani* OMA 6–4 7–6(2) | *Mudrik Al Rawahi* OMA d. *Othman Al Ulama* UAE 6–3 6–4 | *Othman Al Ulama/Omar-Bahrzrouzyan Awadhy* UAE d. *Khalid Al Nabhani/Mudrik Al Rawahi* OMA 7–6(3) 6–4

Saudi Arabia d. Bahrain 2–1

Badar Al Megayel KSA d. *Essam Abdul-Aal* BRN 6–3 6–3 | *Abdullah Nour* KSA d. *Abdul-Rahman Shehab* BRN 7–6(6) 6–4 | *Nader Abdul-Aal/Fahad Sarwani* BRN d. *Omar Al Thagib/Baqer Abu Khulaif* KSA 6–2 6–7(1) 6–1

Jordan d. Fiji 2–1

Ahmad Al Hadid JOR d. *Hitesh Morriswala* FIJ 6–1 6–2 | *Sanjeev Tikaram* FIJ d. *Abdalla Fada* JOR 6–4 7–5 | *Ahmad Al Hadid/Abdalla Fada* JOR d. *Sanjeev Tikaram/Mohammed Jannif* FIJ 6–4 7–6(6)

Oman d. Brunei 3–0

Khalid Al Nabhani OMA d. *Hardiyamin Baharuddin* BRU 6–1 6–0 | *Mudrik Al Rawahi* OMA d. *Billy Wong* BRU 6–0 6–1 | *Khalid Al Nabhani/Mohammed Al Nabhani* OMA d. *Ismasuifian Ibrahim/Billy Wong* BRU 6–3 6–1

Final Positions: 1. Saudi Arabia, 2. Bahrain, 3. Oman, 4. Jordan, 5. Fiji, 6. United Arab Emirates, 7. Brunei | Saudi Arabia and Bahrain promoted to Asia/Oceania Group III in 2001

AFTERWORD

Who would have thought that after fifteen years of playing the sport of tennis—ten of which included representing Australia in Davis Cup—I would play in two Davis Cup Finals in the last two years of my career?

As 1999 came to a close, so too, I thought, were my days of representing my country in this wonderful team competition. I had achieved what I dreamt of as an aspiring youngster back in Adelaide, winning one of sport's famous team competitions for Australia. Unwisely I decided to retire from Davis Cup play at the start of 2000, citing it time for younger guys to take over the reins. Yet, as the first round was underway (Australia began its defense in Switzerland), I found myself doing a clinic in Hawaii, thinking of what my teammates were doing in practice, where they were going for dinner, the laughs had by all, and I discovered I was missing out. I wanted to be there. The second round began against the Germans, and there I was, once more proudly wearing the "green'n'gold" on my back, basking in the feeling of representing my country once again. I had made a mistake and been hasty with my retirement but I was given another opportunity to play.

I remember in 1999, after we beat the Russians in the semifinals, I spoke at our post-team dinner about participating in a Davis Cup Final—what we needed to be aware of in the build-up, the noise during each match, and how we must pull together as a team, as a unit, as one. We managed to achieve that and go on and win against the French. It was a great feeling.

There were no speeches made this year after defeating the Brazilians in the semifinals, as we all knew what was ahead of us. We knew it would be a very tough match against the Spanish and we all went into it as one.

The Final of Davis Cup 2000 was my last match as a professional tennis player. I could have finished in a regular event playing for myself but the chance to loft this great trophy once more was too mouthwatering, to wear the "green'n'gold," to be with my teammates, to play for Australia. That's what Davis Cup is about. We came a little short this year but we made a huge effort and I will always remember what a great team we were.

I will be watching from the sidelines next year as the Aussie team tries to reach a third consecutive Final. It will be hard for me not to be there in person but my thoughts will be with them always and maybe someday I can return to Davis Cup in another role.

Mark Woodforde

ACKNOWLEDGMENTS

When I was approached at the Australian Open 2000 by Barbara Travers from the International Tennis Federation to ask if I'd like to embark on this journey, I had no inkling it would be such a memorable and fulfilling time. My thanks first to Chris Clarey of the *International Herald Tribune* for bequeathing such eminent writings over the past three years—a difficult act to follow.

The participants have delivered rich and fulsome color to my year and I'd like to express special gratitude to those who have given of their time, be they players or captains: Andre Agassi, George Bastl, Alex Corretja, Albert Costa, Roger Federer, Juan Carlos Ferrero, Sebastien Grosjean, Levar Harper-Griffith (we will never forget that visit to the Harare township), Tim Henman, Jakob Hlasek, Gustavo Kuerten, David Lloyd, Fernando Meligeni, John McEnroe, Giovanni Lapentti, Christophe and Olivier Rochus, Roger Taylor, Chris Woodruff, and Mariano Zabaleta. Extra special thanks and g'bye mates, to those proud Aussies John Newcombe, Tony Roche, and Mark Woodforde. May your affection for the Davis Cup stay ever strong. Welcome to the hot seat, John Fitzgerald and Wally Masur.

Thanks, of course, to Jon Ryan, my sports editor at the Sunday Telegraph, for embracing my delight at being given this opportunity and supporting me fully, to my fellow tennis-writing itinerants, especially John Parsons and Barry Flatman from Britain, Leo Schlink from Australia, Vincent Cognet from France, and Jurg Vogel from Switzerland for their brilliant insight.

I must apologize to those smashing people at the ATP for my constant nattering in their ears: Big David Law, Nicola Arzani, Rebecka Hjorth, Martin Dagahs, and Benito Perez-Barbadillo never turned a deaf one when they might have. Thanks to Barbara Travers at the ITF and her terrific assistants, Katie Warburg and Nick Imison. To Pedro Hernandez on behalf of the Spanish Federation, Randy Walker from the USTA, and Lysette Shaw at Tennis Australia: their time and assistance was much appreciated. Jeff Ryan, Mr. Fixit at the USTA, was forever helpful. To Paul Chingoka, ever-genial president at the Zimbabwean Tennis Association, fraternal greetings and thanks for the splendid hospitality.

To the picture men for their continued brilliance, the designers Heather Buckley and Brian Sisco at Two Twelve Associates, and editor Alex Tart at Universe—superb teamwork abounded. I hope they enjoyed this as much as I have. When I needed peace and quiet at home, love and thanks to my wife, Maureen, for finding something to do with my beautiful daughters, Elizabeth and Kathleen. (Promise it will be my turn one day!)

Neil Harman • December 21, 2000